Thinking Children

Also available from Continuum

Philosophy of Education, Richard Pring
Education and Community, Dianne Gereluk
Theory and Practice of Education, David Turner
Values in Education, Graham Haydon
Educational Attainment and Society, Nigel Kettley
Private Education, Geoffrey Walford

Thinking Children

Claire Cassidy

continuum

Continuum International Publishing Group
The Tower Building   80 Maiden Lane, Suite 704
11 York Road   New York, NY 10038
London
SE1 7NX

www.continuumbooks.com

British Library Cataloguing-in-Publication Data
A catalogue record for this book is available from the British Library.

ISBN: 9780826498182 (hardcover)

Library of Congress Cataloging-in-Publication Data
Cassidy, Claire
    Thinking children / Claire Cassidy
        p. cm.
    Includes bibliographical references
ISBN-13: 978-0-8264-9818-2 (hardcover)
ISBN-10: 0-8264-9818-3 (hardcover)
    1. Children. 2. Persons—Philosophy. 3. Children and adults. 4. Children's rights.
I. Title.
    HQ767.9.C376 2007
    305.2301–dc22   2007021960

Typeset by YHT Ltd, London
Printed and bound in Great Britain by Briddles Ltd, Kings Lynn, Norfolk.

Contents

Acknowledgements

There are several individuals and groups of individuals who have made this book possible. I acknowledge the invaluable experiences of facilitating Community of Philosophical Inquiry with a range of groups, including adult community groups and groups of children in schools within Glasgow.

My specific thanks for their work in practical philosophy go to Alistair, Andrew, Ayisha, Catherine, Eitan, John, Mary, Pat, Robert and Ruth for their work in practical philosophy.

Some of the ideas presented in relation to the topic of children as persons appear in *Thinking: Journal of Philosophy for Children*, 2006b, 17(3). I would like to thank the editors of the journal for their kind permission to reproduce these ideas here. Thanks also go to the editors of *Childhood and Philosophy: Journal of the International Council of Philosophical Inquiry with Children*, 2006a, 2(4) for granting their permission to publish the discussion of children as philosophizing citizens presented within this book.

I also wish to thank others who have shared their thinking and support throughout the writing of this book. These thanks go to my parents, Johnny and Helen, my sister, Julie and my friends Aileen, Ann, Claire, Frances, Francis, Garry, Gordon, Janice, Jill, Rebecca, Vesselin and Victoria.

Special thanks for support, guidance and encouragement, as always, go to Donald.

Introduction

Thinking Children investigates the concept of 'child'. In very recent years the subjects of child and childhood have attracted more and more attention. However, the majority of literature on 'child' has been written from an educational, psychological, sociological or historical standpoint. This book differs from what has been written previously in that the concept of child will be considered from a *philosophical* perspective. Little has been written on the topic of 'child' from this position; *Thinking Children* aims to redress this omission. The aim of this book is to come to an acceptable definition of 'child'. In seeking to define what 'child' is, it is anticipated that such a definition will impact upon how those seen as children are perceived in society. Ultimately, there will be implications for the ways in which children are viewed and understood and how they are, therefore, treated within society which will further determine their role and involvement within that society.

Initially, consideration will be given, in Chapter 1, to the notion of 'person' as it will be important to determine just what constitutes a person and his/her personhood in order to ascertain whether or not a child is actually a person in the first instance. The differences between humans and other animals will be considered, if indeed there are any. The discussion on personhood will include some reference to the idea of moral codes. As we exist in a moral world it is necessary that there is some consideration of how our moral codes impact on our personhood. The issue of person as a role concept will be considered and will be linked to the role aspect of child.

In relation to the issue of moral codes and one's personal identity, the main area of concern, as discussed in Chapter 2, will be the 'self'. This will be tied together with the creation of one's identity or 'I' and will be related to the notion of continuous personal identity. Again, the notion of child will be considered during the discussion on continuous personal identity. Before continuing with the argument over morality, personhood and reasoning abilities in terms of children, it is necessary to give some time to reflect upon the historical background of the child and childhood. In order that child can be defined, we must know from where the concept originated and how it has evolved within our society. In Chapter 3 it will be suggested that there is a circularity in the way children have been treated in society as we now seem to be returning to a more medieval approach and treatment of children.

The medieval world saw children and adults functioning within the same social sphere and there is a suggestion that the knowledge gap that was created with the advent of the printing press was reinstated for a while but that this line is becoming more blurred in twenty-first century Western society. The knowledge gap that perpetuated the division of adults and children has allowed the promotion of the idea that children's abilities to articulate their thinking in general and their thinking about their moral codes and the moral codes of others is not likely. Chapter 4 offers some discussion about children's reasoning abilities, and, more specifically, children's reasoning abilities in a philosophical setting.

The subject of personhood is raised again in Chapter 5, but this time in terms of children's personhood. It will be asserted that children are socialized into 'appropriate' or 'acceptable' behaviour for the society to which they belong which will enable conclusions to be drawn about the status of children in society. Again, consideration will be given to children in terms of continuous personal identity.

It is impossible to talk about roles within society, how persons are defined, how status is controlled in relation to children and our expectations of these individuals without reflecting on the notion of the 'citizen' and his/her place within society. The reciprocal nature of citizenship and the rights, duties and responsibilities within one's citizen role will be discussed in Chapter 6. The book posits a model for the promotion and cultivation of active, participative and political citizens. The issue of being reasoning and rational individuals will necessarily be discussed further.

Practical philosophy in the form of Community of Philosophical Inquiry will be given some consideration in Chapter 7, in terms of how it may engender a more positive and reasoning society with the role of the Facilitator in Community of Philosophical Inquiry being discussed and compared to that of Socrates as midwife.

Finally, Chapter 8 will look again at the topics discussed in earlier chapters. Child as citizen is built onto the notion that children should be empowered to be active and participative citizens since they are able and adept reasoners. Some consideration will be given to the place of children's voices in society as it is and as it could be. Here I aim to provide a definition of the concept of 'child' and will posit ways in which this definition may work towards the empowerment of children within society.

Children and adult human beings are placed differently in the social world; through coming to an acceptable definition of child it is the aim of this book to determine whether such differential status is merited in society's treatment of its members. The title of the book, *Thinking Children*, is no accident; the reader is encouraged to think about children and to note that *thinking children* potentially have a very different place and position in society, and one that is more positive, political and participative than at present.

1

The Morality of Personhood

It will be argued here that human beings are animals but that there is something which separates them from other non-human animals. By determining in what ways humans may be different to other animals we may be helped in our understanding of how children differ from adult human beings – if, in fact, they do. It is acknowledged that humans are social animals, but that perhaps what distinguishes this species from others is that humans interact in a very specific way. Human interaction may be manifested through interactions between persons, where persons are those who treat others as such. While individuals may be persons, it will be posited that, equally, they are carrying out a role in society. This person-role is closely linked to accepted social behaviours and relationships. While it will be suggested that we are ascribed the role of person at birth, this book will question in what ways, if at all, children are persons. As personhood is bound by socially acceptable behaviour, this chapter will consider how an individual's moral code, or the prevailing majority moral code, impacts upon society at large. As children exist within society it will be necessary to reflect somewhat upon their roles in society and consideration will be given as to how children are perceived in relation to the notion of person.

From the outset it is important to note that the notion of child is one that is usually considered in terms of becoming, as a transitory stage in one's life on the way to adulthood and full inclusion into society. Jenks (1982a) highlights this view of the child when he says that

From within a variety of disciplines, perspectives and sets of interests childhood receives treatment as a stage, a structural becoming, never as a course of action nor a social practice. The kind of 'growth' metaphors that are used in discussion about children are all of the character of what is yet to be, yet which is also presupposed; thus childhood is spoken of as 'becoming', as a *tabula rasa*, as laying the foundations, taking on, growing up, preparation, inadequacy, inexperience, immaturity, and so on. Such metaphors all seem to speak of a relation to an unexplicated but nevertheless firmly established, rational adult world. This world is not only assumed to be complete and static, but also desirable.

(Jenks, 1982a, p. 13)

So it would appear that the purpose of our being is to be adult and to be fully involved in society as an adult. However, there is no clear explanation of what this entails or how child individuals are different or distinct from adult individuals in relation to their purpose or point of existence. This is what this book aims to redress or resolve; exactly what is the difference – if there is one – between adult and child individuals and how may we define 'child' in light of this? Indeed, Archard suggests that '... it may well be our judgments as to what matters in being an adult which explains why we have the particular conception of childhood we do' (1993, p. 23).

'We are born, so to speak, twice over, born into existence, and born into life; born a human being and born a man,' writes Rousseau (1948, p. 172) in *Emile*. This suggests that being a human being and being a man (or woman) are different things; that there is something to being a man (or woman) that is beyond, or other, to being a human being. Rousseau goes on to state that 'By nature men are neither kings, nobles, courtiers nor millionaires' (*ibid.*, p. 183). He suggests that we should 'Begin with the study of the essentials of humanity, that which really constitutes mankind' (*ibid.*, p. 183). Let us consider, then, what it is that makes us human. What is a human being? What are we human beings 'by nature'?

I is not a Hippo

We are *Homo sapiens*, a distinct species or interbreeding group. As each of us is conceived, we are conceived to *Homo sapiens* parents and in turn, as our parentage is one of a species, we follow suit and are thus born human also. Rousseau, writing in the eighteenth century said that 'Before his parents chose a calling for him [Emile] nature called him to be a man' (*ibid.*, p. 9). And although parents nowadays rarely select the career path of their offspring, it remains true that nature in the first instance determines that one is a human animal.

Ruse holds that '... what really makes us humans successful as a species is our ability to interact socially with our fellows' (1995, p. 375). We exist as a social group. In the main, we rely on those others within our species to aid us in our daily existences, whether they be parent, shop assistant, police officer or friend. We, as humans, interact and depend upon that interaction with other individuals belonging to our group. Taylor talks about Chrysippus' suggestion that while 'Humans have the same sensuous impulses (*hormetikai phantasiai*) as animals ... they are not forced to act on them' (1989, p. 137). Certainly humans want to eat, sleep, procreate, even fight. These impulses or desires cannot be denied the human animal any more than they be denied a lion, dog, mouse or hippopotamus. However, as Chrysippus would argue, we – as active human agents – 'are not forced to act on them'. There is something which separates, or makes us different from the other beasts of our communal planet, there is something that restrains us from wantonly following our animal urges, there is something more, an added ingredient in the soup of our make up that enables us to function on a level different to the hippo, mouse, dog or lion.

It can be said that in everyday human activity there is a dis-similarity between human beings and the rest of the animal world and that the evidence for this is not only to be seen, but also, it could be argued, that the sensation we humans experience is *felt* – we actively hold back on our 'sensuous impulses'. There is something that stops me tearing off the clothes of the attractive man in the seat beside me in the darkened cinema to engage in the most animal of impulses; but what is it that stops me? If I were a hippo on a South African game reserve nothing would stop that animal magnetism being fulfilled; so there I am in the cinema, but the handsome man beside me remains untouched – why? Where is the hippo in me?

Perhaps what separates me from the hippo is the way in which I behave towards the other individual. I treat him in a certain way, in a manner which would not occur to the hippo. My treatment of another would involve behaviour which is more than living in a group for the sake of finding food and procreation; I behave towards others as though they are more important or valued than mere providers of food or as partners in the production of babies. In other words, I behave towards others as though they were *persons*. I would posit that a person learns to think of him/herself as a person when others react to him/her as such. We, in a collective sense, are more than human animals; we are, it seems, also persons. From the first, I would suggest that 'person' is not synonymous with other labels often used interchangeably by philosophers and people in general, such as human being, individual, self, I, citizen, and so on; it is an additional part of being within a human context.

Persons

Persons are human beings. This initial statement does not necessarily hold in reverse – human beings may not always be persons. What, then, does it mean to treat someone as a person? 'Person' is seen as a positive attribute. We all want to be seen as persons and treated as such; Downie and Telfer concur; '... the concept of *person* is already an evaluative concept with something of the force of "that which makes a human being valuable" implied in it' (1969, p. 19). Therefore, in treating another individual as a person, we are valuing them in some sense. Kant emphasizes that in order to treat someone as a person one should behave towards him/her as an end in him/herself. He holds that

Persons, therefore, are not merely subjective ends whose existence as an object of our actions has a value *for us*: they are *objective ends* – that is, things whose existence is in itself an end, and indeed an end such that in its place we can put no other end to which they should serve *simply* as means.

(Kant, 1989, p. 91)

He goes on to state this more succinctly in his 'practical imperative'; 'Act in such a way that you always treat humanity, whether in your own person or in the person of any other, never simply as a means, but always at the same time as an end' (*ibid.*, p. 91).

Perhaps, as Elkin and Handel posit, the first experience we have of being treated as a person is within the family; 'Since children's first social relationships are family relationships, it is in this group that they acquire their first experiences of being treated as persons in their own right' (1978, p. 122). There is a problem here, however. Certainly one would hope that the child or infant is being valued as an end in itself, yet, one may wonder whether the infant is being treated 'as a person' in order to generate a desired outcome, an individual who will play an appropriate part in society – whatever appropriate means in such a context. To use MacMurray's example of a master and his slave and then relate it to children and parents and the wider family circle:

It [the relation of a master to his slave] is constituted by the intention of the master to treat the other person 'as a means merely' ... Consequently he regards him not as a person, nor as an agent, but as an object possessing certain capacities and characteristics which make him useful.

(MacMurray, 1970, p. 34)

If we consider the reasons people give for having children, it can be seen that children are viewed very much like the slave in MacMurray's example. For instance, a child may be conceived in order to make a family 'complete', to give either one of the partners a 'purpose', as an expression or symbol of the partners' love for one another, to carry on the family line or to provide tissue or cells to aid the survival of another sibling. If one were to raise the issue of the unplanned pregnancy, it would be no different. In all of these examples the newborn is not seen as an end in itself, but as a means to an end. However, the child may not be so innocent itself.

Harre suggests that

> ... by copying their every word and gesture as best he can, a baby seems to be treating those around him as persons [and] among the ways of speaking and acting that a baby imitates is the way in which other people treat him as a person.
>
> (Harre, 1987, p. 101)

Consciously or not, the baby is not treating others as persons if that means treating them as ends rather than as means to an end; he/she is using the individuals around him/herself to learn how to interact and behave in the world. He/she needs the others in order to function in that society; a baby '... can only live through other people and in dynamic relation with them' (MacMurray, 1970, p.51), he/she uses them for his/her own ends. In fact, all babies and certainly the majority of younger individuals rely solely on their older counterparts to provide for them in terms of food, clothing, shelter, guidance, and so on. Yet is the child in this scenario any different from any other individual in society? No. Like the baby, or child, other individuals use one another as a gauge of behaviour or as a guide for participating in society or to learn from, it is merely the case that those we know of as children need a starting point because they have less experience of living, that they perhaps take more from others in terms of needing to be socialized.

Additionally, humans are social in nature, their communities and societies are based on the need for others, and others are not just needed for the sake of being, they are needed because of what they can do or provide for us as individuals or for the larger social group – they are, in many ways, a means to an end – our end. However, this does not take away from the fact that they are valued in some sense – even if it is for what they will contribute to our society.

Similarly, it may be posited that children are valued for what they will *become*, although this fails to meet the criteria of valuing them as they are *now* for *what* they are now. In the positive and valuing ways parents behave towards their offspring one might suggest that they are treating them as persons. They take care of their needs; the child is fed, clothed, given protection, given language and communication skills, provided with social skills and some form of education. However, again this seems to be more concerned with the child in terms of its future adult life – what it will *become*.

Perhaps we need to consider the problem the other way round; it may be the case that it is in *treating* others as valuable individuals that makes one a person. In order to be a person one must treat others in a positive and valued way. So it is not so much that one is being treated as a person that makes one a person, but that in behaving towards someone else as a person one becomes or maintains a personhood. It is relatively simple to behave towards others in society – whatever their age – in a positive way, in a way which demonstrates some value for their being, but there are instances where this may not be such a simple situation. If we consider those who have broken the law and have been punished by being placed in prison, do we consider such individuals to be persons? While such an individual may not have treated others as persons, in that they did not value them, but instead used them for their own personal gain with complete disregard for the individuals concerned as ends in themselves, merely as a means, then they perhaps lose their personhood. However, society – and those particularly responsible for running our prisons and other institutions for punishing those who break the law – are *bound* to treat the inmates as persons. The prisoners must be fed, clothed and given shelter, they must be treated as valued individuals, not to make them persons, but in order that the care-givers may maintain *their* personhood. There is a sense of obligation or duty implied here on the part of the provider, but also one must question whether the criminal was ever a person or if they could ever regain their personhood or attain it for the first time. The same is true for children; the parents – or carers – are persons so long as they are treating the child in a positive and valued manner, but the child does not become a person because they are being treated as such.

One should perhaps note the linguistic use of treating an individual *as* a person. There is an assumption that a particular individual is a person and we relate to him/her as though that were the case, but until there is evidence that he/she can treat or behave towards other individuals as though they are persons, then personhood is denied or in some sense held in reserve. One may be nominally a person by being treated *as* a person without having demonstrated one's personhood in his/her treatment of others. This is certainly an attribute animals other than humans do not have. Animals do not behave towards others as though they were persons, as though they were valuable in and of themselves. However, there are occasions when animals are treated *as* persons. The way in which we behave towards our pets suggests that we treat them as we would other individuals we value; we feed them, play with them, exercise them, talk to them and worry about their welfare – we behave towards them as though our behaviour will be, or could be, reciprocated. So, where does this notion of person come from and when does one acquire this personhood – in the nominal, yet to be proven, sense?

Rorty (1976a) suggests that

> Our idea of persons derives from ... the *dramatis personae* of the stage ... An actor dons masks, literally *per sonae*, that through which sound comes, the many roles he acts. A person's roles and his place in the narrative devolve from the choices that place him in a structural system, related to others. The person thus comes to stand behind his roles, to select them and to be judged by his choices and his capacities to act out his personae in a total structure that is the unfolding of his drama.
>
> (Rorty, 1976a, p. 309)

This notion of the *dramatis personae* places us firmly on the social stage which involves us in 'playing our part'; we adopt the role and thus function in society among others who are equally utilizing their roles to participate. Schrag (1997) affirms our social standing:

Just as the characters in the narratives of literary invention mark out the roles of the protagonists and the *dramatis personae* in the epic, the novel, the short story, and the drama, so the characteristics that constitute self-identity in everyday life mark out the roles of speakers and hearers, authors and readers, as they each achieve their respective stances within a panoply of communicative practices.

(Schrag, 1997, P.39)

So, can we take personhood to be a role? Is it a mantle we adopt or maintain in order to preserve some status in society among the other inhabitants?

The Person Role

Downie would agree that personhood is something additional to being a human animal; he states that '... "person" is not the same as the biological notion of an individual human animal, but is an institutional notion' (1971, p. 131). Certainly our laws are laid down by institutions – or at least the representatives elected to be in such institutions and we, it may be argued, adopt this institutional role in order to function within the parameters set by such establishments or individuals which constitute society. Institution, here, is seen as a governing body, be that a parliamentary, political, educational, familial body; the rule is consistent, these people set the moral codes in some sense, although it is only parliamentarians who are formally elected by the body of participatory citizens. However, one could extrapolate and say the likes of teachers or the police (but not parents) are elected in the sense that they have met the criteria set out under which they are permitted to accept the responsibility of being this type of 'enforcer' of moral codes.

Downie has gone on to say that

... if it means [to speak of the *ergon*, function or role of a person] that a given individual is an X, Y, Z *and a person* (where 'person' is put in the same list as other roles) then the concept of person is distorted, and the concept of role is trivialized.

(*ibid.*, p. 132)

On the contrary, it is simply because we human beings use the term 'person' in a non-pejorative sense that it is seen as a positive accreditation that Downie, in this instance, would not see it as distorted or trivialized – and Downie himself was previously seen to hold that 'person' implied something of value. MacIntyre (1999) discusses that in the classical tradition

> ... to be a man is to fill a set of roles each of which has its own point and purpose: member of a family, citizen, soldier, philosopher, servant of God. It is only when man is thought of as an individual prior to and apart from all roles that 'man' ceases to be a functional concept.
>
> (MacIntyre, 1999, p. 59)

...and the notion of person sees and treats 'man' as more than a functional concept. As a person, which society generally considers us to be, one would not like to be seen as a non-person or not a person. Downie argues his case stating that '... to say all this is not to say that "person" simply names another role. If person is a role-concept – it is not in the same category as other roles; it cannot be, since it cannot be *chosen*' (1971, p. 132). There are roles, however, that one equally cannot choose; I cannot choose to be a sister; I cannot choose to be a daughter; if I have a child I become a mother. So, although I cannot *choose* to be a person and am assigned the role, I will learn the expected part and behaviour that accompanies it.

Certainly the notion of person is an attribute, it is a given role and it is given at birth. Parsons links this idea with that of the socializing of children, '... *the socializee* must be conceived as acting in roles. At the instant of birth, perhaps, the infant does not do so. But almost immediately a role is ascribed to him which includes expectations of his behaviour' (1982, p. 140). The role the child is expected to adopt when ascribed its first role is as an individual who is innocent and lacks power. Jenks highlights this perception when he says that the child is seen as '... innately innocent, confirming its cultural identity as a passive and unknowing dependent, and therefore as a member of a social group utterly disempowered' (1996, p. 124). Jenks emphasizes how much the child's role is categorized and determined:

Routinely, children find their daily lives shaped by statuses regulating the pacing and placing of their experience. Compulsory schooling, for example, restricts their access to social space and gerontocratic prohibitions limit their political involvement, sexual activity, entertainment and consumption.

(*ibid.*, p.122)

In fact, the role of the child at this time is merely to learn the behaviour of the society in which he/she finds him/herself. Durkheim (1982) indicates what he perceives the child's role to be:

The essential function of this age, the role and purpose assigned to it by nature, may be summed up in a single word: it is the period of *growth*, that is to say, the period in which the individual, in both the physical and moral sense, does not yet exist, the period in which he is made, develops and is formed.

(Durkheim, 1982, p. 146)

This socialization process is one which prepares the child for its future life as an adult; again we meet the child as a means to an end.

The role of learner is subtly influenced, and one of the easiest ways to role play is through giving the young individual toys to learn through. Barthes (1982) holds that

All the toys one sees are essentially a microcosm of the adult world; they are all reduced copies of human objects ... The fact that French toys *literally* prefigure the world of adult functions obviously cannot but prepare the child to accept them all, by constituting for him, even before he can think about it, the alibi of a Nature which has at all times created soldiers, postmen and Vespas. Toys here reveal the list of all the things the adult does not find unusual: war; bureaucracy, ugliness, Martians, etc.

(Barthes, 1982, p. 134)

Here children are given the opportunity, with toys, to practise their future adult role, and – more especially – the role of person, as they must interact and relate to the other individuals within the scene, employing the toys *as* persons. Using the tools of play the child can adopt the person role in the way he/she behaves towards the others – real or imagined – in the play. Children are not set apart here; adults similarly are shaped in their roles, as Downie and Telfer (1969) suggest:

> ...it is not just that we are in some external way moulded by the social roles we adopt, but rather that our very identity as persons is constituted by the relationships in which we are placed by our social roles.

> (Downie and Telfer 1969, p.31)

We should not forget that personhood is a social role; there needs to be others in our society in order for one to be a person and or for others to maintain that role. MacIntyre lists some of the roles we inhabit: 'I am someone's son or daughter, someone else's cousin or uncle; I am a citizen of this or that city, member of this or that clan, that tribe, this nation' (1999, p. 220). He continues:

> Hence what is good for me has to be the good for one who inhabits these roles. As such, I inherit from the past of my family, my city, my tribe, my nation, a variety of debts, inheritances, rightful expectations and obligations. These constitute the given of my life, my moral starting point. This is in part what gives my life its own moral particularity.

> (*ibid.*, p. 220)

It may be argued that in everything we do we are acting in role, be that as a person or one of the roles listed by MacIntyre, but, whatever the role, it must take place in a social context, and if we are expected to maintain the role of person in this social context – for who would want to rid oneself of it deliberately – then the notion is bound up with how we treat others – and so, it is a moral concept. This 'person' is '... a locus of responsibility for a range of choices and actions' (Rorty, 1976a, p. 309) and exists in a society.

Put very simply, a society is made up of people living in close proximity to one another; Giddens defines it as '... a *system of interrelationships* which connects individuals together' (1993, p. 32), and expands his definition by later adding that society is '... a group of people who live in a particular territory, are subject to a common system of political authority, and are aware of having a distinct identity from other groups around them' (*ibid.*, p. 746) – this is how the term will be used in this book. I would agree with Perkins that '... men exist in society and are determined to a large degree by this fact; biological expectations are not sufficient to describe the nature of man, even psychological ones must be supplemented by sociological principles' (1969, p. 82). So, this group that forms a society is bound by some sociological principles, principles we will here call rules. They, those members of a society, are bound by – and live by – an agreed 'moral code'.

Moral Codes

What is meant by the term 'moral code'? Moral codes are the rules or regulations which we hold in terms of what is good/bad or right/wrong. We each have a personally held system of these beliefs or codes which influence the ways in which we interact and participate with others in our society. Some may choose to call this moral code a conscience. Perkins suggests that Condillac would be one such philosopher. He maintains that we are born with a conscience; '... *conscience* is implicit in sensation; the former is both genetically and logically prior to the latter. The thought of any kind of sense impression existing without a conscious mind to receive it was inconceivable to Condillac' (1969, p. 54). Rousseau would seem to concur when he states in *Emile* that 'We are born sensitive and from our birth onwards we are affected in various ways by our environment' (1948, p. 7). Before we encounter much of life with other individuals, before we have a full grasp of the intricacies of the social life in which humans engage, we have a sensitivity, it is suggested here, some built-in mechanism we use to relate to our environment, which will ultimately govern our behaviour in the society into which we have been born. This, again, may be something which sets humans apart from the rest of the animal kingdom; they (other animals) do not appear to have consciences. This conscience is a tool that is used to help us decide the good from the bad, the right from the wrong. Aristotle holds that this is a natural aptitude, that we are born with a capacity for knowing right from wrong; 'We must be born with an eye for a moral issue which will enable us to form a correct judgement and choose what is truly good' (1955, p. 92). It is not Nature, according to Aristotle, that gives us these moral virtues which we live by, but it is Nature that prepares us for knowing what is right or wrong when we encounter it and we learn through experience of the world and people around us what is acceptable and what is not. Rousseau (1948) would maintain that we innately recognize right from wrong and the tool we use for deciding such is the conscience:

> There are therefore at the bottom of our hearts innate principles of justice and virtue, by which ... we judge our own actions or those of others to be good or evil; and it is this principle that I call conscience.
>
> (Rousseau, 1948, p. 252)

The individual may be unable to articulate the whys and wherefores of what he/she believe to be right/wrong, good/bad; he/she may not even be able to engage in dialogue or to reason about the subject. As is often the case, the individual may only be able to say that they *feel* something to be right; they know it is how things should – or should not – be, but cannot explain why they should feel or believe something to be so. One illustration of this point may be when a child is experiencing abuse; he/she does not talk about it, has never discussed it, yet from the outset has believed or known it to be wrong.

Then where do we get the morality our conscience recognizes? Mayo (1986) suggests that

> All that it is really safe to say is that morality is *acquired* and *imparted*; that we do become more or less decent men and women as a result of

some early processing: by some form of interaction between ourselves and others who already have their moral standards and practices.

(Mayo, 1986, p. 2)

We adopt certain beliefs or codes as our own and apply them to our lives – as Downie (1971) suggests, first

> ...a person must decide for himself what he believes to be morally right if his beliefs are to count as moral beliefs at all. Hence, moral views seem to be in some sense irreducibly subjective or peculiar to the moral agent who holds them.
>
> (Downie, 1971, p.12)

We cannot suppose, however, that society is able to function via a series of subjective beliefs. While it has been suggested that we all have moral codes in that we are all able to decide what we believe to be right or wrong, good or bad and that this shapes *our* behaviour, there must be some acknowledgement that we are not in a society of one and that not everyone's moral codes will concur. Mayo posits 'All that is needed for me to judge that one moral code is better than another is that I should *have* a moral code; not that there should be an "absolute" code as well' (1986, p. 84). We have to acknowledge that we will have beliefs or codes that we choose to live by and would elect that if the opportunity arose, society would function along a code it shares with us. However, what is important is that we *have* a code which we follow and that others have a different code. This is important in order that society evolves, but we should have some conviction about the way in which our particular society is run. Society itself can only be shaped by those acting consciences, but society can be a coherent functioning entity when these moral notions are accepted by the whole group; at the same time, society can become fractious, torn apart even, when conflicting consciences collide – and it cannot be legislated that humans are all born with an agreed conviction of what makes something good or bad, right or wrong. The actual rights or wrongs, goods or evils are irrelevant in the argument. The fact is that there are those who, within a society, agree what is good or right and there are those who would disagree. The point is that it is this very disagreement that causes conflict within a society or smaller social group, and this is what causes discord and ultimately maintains the ever-changing society within which we find ourselves. In this society, then, we have to interact with other individuals whose moral codes may differ by twists and turns with our own, but it is this social interaction that prompts us to espouse our own moral codes.

Hobbes (1949) suggests that

> Theft, murder, adultery and all injuries are forbid by the laws of nature; but what is it to be called theft, what murder, what adultery, what injury in a citizen, this is not to be determined by the natural, but by the civil law.

> (Hobbes, 1949, p.81)

While our belief systems and moral codes are subjective in that we have our own perspectives and understandings of things and are shaped by these understandings and codes, there needs to be some form of objectivity in order that society functions effectively. It cannot be assumed that each individual will hold the same moral code. Society is forming, controlling, constraining or directing the individuals within that society by articulating the moral codes of the majority and enforcing them in the form of laws or regulations. Shields looks to Wittgenstein when he says 'To obey a rule, to make a report, to give an order, to play a game of chess, are customs.' He adds 'In other words, practices require a *history* of agreement in behaviour among a community of practitioners, and this is what gives the practice normative force' (1998, p. 172). In a democracy there is a formalized method of establishing rules which represent the moral codes and beliefs of the majority of the population – the majority of those individuals that have the entitlement to vote. Hobbes (1949) holds that

> Democracy is not framed by a contract of particular persons with people, but by mutual compacts of single men each with other. But

hence, it appears, in the first place, that the persons contracting must be in being before the contract itself.

(Hobbes, 1949, p. 91)

It is assumed, then, that the individuals constituting society are in the first place persons and behave towards others as though they too were persons in order that the contract of following the majority moral code is enacted – albeit this agreement is unspoken.

In British democracy the majority elects, from its group, a representative to formalize its moral codes into a set of governing laws. This representative is not solely representational in the sense that he/she is another from the species to which the society belongs – a human being – but the elected individual holds a moral outlook that corresponds with the group that have elected him or her as its representative. In the society within which we in Britain function, we listen to these individuals' moral codes when they seek to represent us and we vote or elect the individual whose code resonates most strongly with our own. We do this in the hope that our representative will receive the majority of votes and will be in a position to be part of the group governing our country, giving voice to and formalizing the moral codes we hold dear and would have others hold. It is acknowledged that it is the case that not every individual has permission or an entitlement to vote, but this too is one of the moral codes made into legislation by our representatives. As Downie (1971) states,

> Sooner or later the Government of a democracy must go to the people, who then have the opportunity to participate indirectly in the process of government by voting into power that party the general aims of which they regard as most nearly fulfilling their own.

(Downie, 1971, p. 102)

He goes on to say that

> ...we expect the Government to represent our moral values by enacting its policies, internationally as well as domestically, in a manner which recognizes interests extending beyond its frontiers,

shows respect for persons ... and indicates an awareness of the importance of moral ideals.

(*ibid.*, p. 114)

The Government is charged with the responsibility of carrying our moral codes into the wider sphere of society, and in so doing must behave for the individuals who compose this society in a positive manner by treating them as persons. Generally speaking, we give the individuals who participate in this electoral system the name or label or role 'citizen', but as not every individual is permitted or desires to take part in this electoral system, we cannot maintain that society is solely made up of citizens; however, it is still possible to be a non-voting citizen if one chooses to participate toward the good of society in other ways. It is suggested here that complementing the notion of person as one who treats others as valued individuals, it is our acceptance of living by these rules, regulations and moral codes created by the majority that makes us persons as this involves treating others in a particular way. When one group with conscience or moral code type A meet another group with conscience or moral code type B, there is conflict, and that conflict must be resolved if the society or community is to survive and be preserved as it is. It could be the case that conscience/code type A who have been in the majority and have legislated the moral code as it is are no longer in the majority and conscience/code type B band together to form a new majority – or very powerful and persuasive minority – and therefore oust the code-writers and themselves take on the mantle of power. However, this does not make conscience/code type B individuals non-persons.

It is our adherence to these sociological principles which goes towards making us persons. This *person* is expected to grow and mature within society. Not only will the individual grow and mature, it is hoped that he/she will become a participative member in that society. And in order to participate 'acceptably' one must have agreed to live by the majority moral code that is at that time governing one's being in that community, be that majority parental, educational, legal, and so on. By agreeing, one accepts that he/she should abide by the code of the moral majority and will therefore recognize the accepted practices, rules, customs or behaviours. There is no formal way to accept this way of living among others; it is assumed that in being born into a certain society one will adhere to the rules set down. It is precisely because individuals have conflicting moral codes that this is not a static situation, but a process whereby the moral majority has the potential to shift from time to time. In discussing the rules a community or society holds and lives by, and its reciprocal nature in terms of behaviour for those within it, MacMurray (1970) states that

> For any member of the community this [the moral orthodoxy or outlook of that community] will define what is expected of him as a moral agent by the community. It will generally, though not necessarily, define what it is right for him to do. Not necessarily, because his own moral apperception – that is, his conscience – may not be identical with the normal one; but generally, otherwise the moral orthodoxy in question would not be normal. Even where the conscience of the individual is unorthodox, however, it must be related to the orthodox code. For morality refers to the structure of personal relations which unites the members in a community of agents, and personal relations are necessarily reciprocal. What is expected of me by the Other must always play an important part ... in determining the morality of my actions.
>
> (MacMurray, 1970, p. 120)

From this it could be argued that society shapes the individual – and to a certain extent it does, but in order to avoid a chicken and egg type argument, one must remember that the moral codes established as law were created by thinking human beings who already had *some* idea of what they held to be good/bad, right/wrong; it could not simply have been learned from the previous generations of that particular society as this would infinitely regress, and the initial notions of morality had to have come from somewhere. Downie sees the need for a consensus in terms of expected and acceptable behaviour in order for society to function well; 'People must know what sort of behaviour to expect of others in their daily lives and they must be able to feel akin to others. In short, in a healthy society there must be moral consensus' (1971, p. 109).

So, at birth we are given the role of person, we have no say – as Downie posited, we cannot choose the role of person – we cannot even at the moment of birth accept it, but we are labelled 'persons' and as such are expected to conform in our moral outlook and behaviour with those others within our community who have already agreed to abide by the codes. We are 'encouraged' in this endeavour by our peers, our parents, teachers, employers, the media, and so on; constant reinforcements abound. I would, therefore, agree here with Downie in considering the roles we adopt in terms of functioning in society when he suggests that

> A role in the relevant sense ... is a cluster of rights and duties with some sort of social function. We can in fact view society as a highly complex set of institutions each of which consists of one or more clusters of rights and duties.
>
> (*ibid.*, p. 128)

Our function as persons is to make the actual mechanisms of society work. As persons we adhere to the underlying codes set out, and in maintaining the status quo society functions well and rewards us with certain entitlements, sometimes called rights.

Downie poses the suggestion that even when one thinks there are no moral claims upon him/her, he/she is still a moral agent and that if one expects to be part of society and accept any benefits or rights afforded to those others in society then certain things are expected in terms of behaviour:

> In so far as a person is capable of moral agency (that is, is rational and able to choose), and in so far as by living in a social group he derives benefits, he is in general terms obliged by the rules of society.
>
> (*ibid.*, p. 130)

MacIntyre (1999) too supports the notion that our actions within society are important and that privileges do not descend upon us without being obliged to behave or act in some way. He holds that a man should be judged by his actions, that there is more than a set of expected duties or privileges and that we are required to act in order to reap these benefits:

> By performing actions of a particular kind in a particular situation a man gives warrant for judgment upon his virtues and vices; for the virtues just are those qualities which sustain a free man in his role and which manifest themselves in those actions which his role requires.
>
> (MacIntyre, 1999, p. 122)

Certainly, in acting within society we will be judged worthy – or not – of the rights allowed those who reside within a society. There are many who complain about unemployed people receiving financial support from the relevant government departments when they consider that these people are not *doing* anything to alter their situation in order that they may contribute to society. Similarly, asylum seekers find themselves in the peculiar position whereby they cannot, in a formal sense, contribute to the society in which they find themselves; however, they are treated as persons in that the society provides for them in terms of providing certain standards of care and education. Such individuals are judged by their actions – or inaction (however involuntary) – by those others within society and this is perhaps not the way to consider the dilemma of personhood. MacMurray suggests that 'An action is defined by its intention, and its absolute rightness must lie, therefore, in the rightness of its intention' (1970, p. 116).

We have already posited that in order to be a person one must behave towards others as though they too were persons, in other words as valued individuals, and additionally, one should abide by the rules of the society within which one finds oneself. Is it now the case that another criterion must be added? Are not merely our actions to be judged, but also the intention lying behind those actions? Certainly, if one is to treat others as ends in themselves, then one should always intend only good for them and the rest of society, and thus in *intending* good it is hoped that the action itself will be good. We are, of course, bound to consider our actions or behaviours within a context and this must contribute in some way to our intentions. If I help an old woman across the road, is it a right action? My intention is to be of assistance, of some help to the lady who cannot cross the busy road herself; we do so successfully and I am rewarded with a feeling of having done the right thing. I intended help and this is what was achieved; no mention has been made of my motivation. Perhaps I knew the old woman would give me a packet of sweets or leave me a fortune in her will for my act of kindness; this is not at issue, I *intended* help. Similarly, rights or entitlements work in much the same way. A certain type of behaviour is required of individuals in society who wish to be seen – and treated – as persons, their intentions may be the best in terms of treating others as ends in themselves, and so we have rights as some kind of inducement to this positive behaviour – these act like the old lady's motivation of a packet of Jelly Babies for my assistance in taking her across the road. Indeed, Aristotle (1986) would appear to agree that it is not the motivation that is rewarded but the actual act itself when he says

> We are not spoken of as good or bad in respect of our feelings but of our virtues and vices. Neither are we praised or blamed for the way we feel ... But we *are* praised or blamed for our virtues and vices.
>
> (Aristotle, 1986, p. 63)

Losing Personhood

In *Utilitarianism* Mill (1972) also highlights that cooperating and considering the needs and feelings of others makes us more empathetic and more willing to work towards the ends of the interests of the others in order to generate a more cohesive society. However, Aristotle also points out that if '... it is in our power to perform an action when it is right, it will equally be in our power to refrain from performing it when it is wrong' (1986, p. 89). Let us remember that not everyone will agree on what is right or correct or acceptable, we have only agreed to abide by the moral code of the majority, the code the rules of our society follows. So, an individual has the potential – and the ability – *not* to act in the accepted manner; he/she is able to break the accepted code and act according to the one he/she personally holds.

So, while one is a person in that he/she agrees to abide by the legislated rules, he/she may equally cease to be a person by dropping or resigning the role in order to act in the manner that resonates with his/her own code. And here the *intention* still holds good, as one would maintain that the actions are still being carried out for the betterment of society as a whole. As Mayo claims 'One can't admit that something is wrong while saying in the same breath that one doesn't care whether it is or not' (1986, p. 13). In fact, in being given the role of person at birth, one is not accepting it; what it means is that in order to *not* be a person in a certain society then one must *reject* the established moral code. And this is precisely where and when conflict happens. Downie (1971) expands upon this idea that moral codes be used for the interests, betterment or good of a society:

> The existence of rules makes generally known the types of action which are conducive to majority interests. Moral rules as a result come to be backed by sanctions. Where the rules are basic to continued stability they may be incorporated in a legal system and supported by the threat of legal sanctions, and they will in any case be backed by social approval and disapproval.
>
> (Downie, 1971, p. 37)

So, we have seen that in maintaining society's rules and regulations one is rewarded in terms of rights and entitlements, however, in breaking the codes of a society one is likely to suffer punishment, retribution or sanctions as a result. In Rousseau's mind, we are free to do this:

> ...for by a right which nothing can abrogate, every man, when he comes of age, becomes his own master, free to renounce the contract by which he forms part of the community, by leaving the country in which that contract holds good.
>
> (Rousseau, 1948, p. 419)

Certainly, it is one option to leave the society if one believes the moral code is too far removed from one's own, however, there are other ways to rescind one's agreement and one way to do this is to lose or abdicate one's personhood. Indeed, one cannot help but be a moral agent; it may just be that one's moral perspective differs from that of the majority:

> ...one cannot choose to reject morality, for an apparent choice not to be a moral agent would still be a disguised moral choice; people who say they are rejecting morality are simply rejecting a given morality.
>
> (Downie, 1971, p. 130)

While one is ascribed his/her personhood at birth, one can have it taken away also; although this may have detrimental effects on the personhood of the punisher. Dennett (1976) considers the notion of personhood in terms of doing wrong or breaking the rules or codes of a society:

> ...our assumption that an entity is a person is shaken precisely in those cases ... when wrong has been done and the question of responsibility arises. For in these cases the grounds for saying that the person is culpable (the evidence that he did wrong, was aware he was doing wrong, and did wrong of his own free will) are in themselves grounds for doubting that it is a person we are dealing with at all.
>
> (Dennett, 1976, p. 194)

Of course, there are some relatively clear demarcations in terms of legal punishment. Earlier in the chapter Hobbes was cited to illustrate that 'crimes' such as murder and theft require definition by civil law, and similarly, punishment is meted out by civil law. However, Mayo (1986) questions the fact of there being a 'moral sentence' or punishment. He suggests that while there is no formal method or procedure for sanctioning such an offender

> ...we can find an analogy in things like social disapproval, ostracism, moral censure, withdrawal of friendship – these look like external

sanctions – and perhaps there are internal ones, such as the unpleasant feeling we call remorse or a guilty conscience.

(Mayo, 1986, p. 64)

This is perhaps some way towards what is entailed in removing or altering someone's personhood; the only problem here though – and this holds with the earlier example of individuals being placed in prison – is that in removing the personhood of another we cease to treat them as a person and in so behaving we are equally losing our own personhood.

Conclusions

It has been argued that in order to be a person one must behave towards others as though they were persons, and that we should also abide by the majority moral code in its drive for the good of society. If we wish to break an agreed moral code, we can break the contract by leaving the society for which the code pertains, but ultimately we cannot be stripped of our personhood as this would alter the status of the individual meting out the punishment. Perhaps all we can say is that if one breaks or fails to keep a code, for example, in killing another individual or taking something belonging to another individual without that individual's consent then one will be punished in a way that will not affect one's personhood, but some *other* aspect of one's being.

When Rousseau embarked upon his 'Reveries', he stated 'I am henceforth nothing among men, and that is all I can be, no longer having any real relations or true society with them' (1979, p. 6). While having no interaction with others Rousseau would consider himself as nothing; he is still, however, an individual with a conscience, a sense of right and wrong. He is still a human being, and until such times as he breaks a moral code – even in his society of one (although he is setting the moral code) – he is still a person; a person acting out the behaviour required of one who wishes to participate in the society or community into which one was born or placed. Consider Downie (1971) when he says that

... however much the rights and duties of the role affect a given action the morality of the action is never wholly reducible to the rights and duties of the role; there is always an irreducibly personal element in any moral action, and a person cannot completely transfer the moral responsibility for what he does to his role.

(Downie, 1971, p. 133)

While I disagree with Downie when he holds that person is not a role, I would agree that our actions are not merely attributable to a role, be that the role of person or citizen. There is something else which we are that again separates us from the 'beasts'.

MacIntyre offers a solution as to where one may find the locus of our morality – if that is what separates us from the animals – if it is not to be found in 'persons'; he claims that we are moral agents and '... it is in the self and not in the social roles or practices that moral agency has to be located' (1999, p. 32). Penelhum (1976) concurs; he allows that one may contribute to society and may have actions in the past that were against the moral code. However, he offers a way of viewing our moral choices in the self and suggests

A person is best able to make his contribution to a changing society if he is not emotionally burdened by his past. Here then, we have excellent moral grounds for changing the temporal boundaries of the self. If we drew these boundaries more narrowly we could generate a convention in which a middle-aged man's youthful actions were classified roughly as the actions of his immediate ancestor are now classified: as the deeds of an earlier self.

(Penelhum, 1976, p. 271)

So, in this chapter it has been argued that a person is not someone who is treated as a person, but is someone who *treats* others *as* persons. Animals do not behave like this and so cannot be persons, although they are often treated as though they are persons. Children are assumed to be able to treat others as persons, and so they are attributed with the personhood role until they are able to prove they can act in the accepted manner. It has been shown that children are more often than not considered in terms of their becoming and as a result adults are not treating children as ends in themselves, but as a means to an end. In maintaining one's personhood one is expected to abide by the majority moral code. We each have a conscience, an ability to determine right from wrong and good from bad, but children are often – usually – not given credence for being able to utilize this faculty, and this is because they have not been fully socialized. In order to consider a definition of child it is important that we pursue the question of morality and its locus within the human being – adult or child.

2

From the Self Comes I

It was suggested at the end of Chapter 1 that morality may be placed somewhere other than in personhood, since personhood is itself a moral concept in that it pertains to our behaviours. In this chapter the notion of self and its relation to morality and our identity will be considered. It will be posited that the self is the internal device which goes some way toward creating the I or identity one has as a human animal, a device other animals do not have, unlike consciousness which is a common feature of all animals. The reflexive nature of the self will be given some consideration, as will the idea that one must complete a lifetime in order to assess one's self. Links will be made to memory and the idea of continuity in terms of one's personal identity in relation to the concept of child. As humans exist in a moral society and as humans are seen to be reasoning and rational beings who reflect upon the moral acts within their society then some discussion will be given over to our reasoning being influential in the creation of our identities, and how this separates *some* of us from the 'beasts'.

The Self

Let us consider the self. Perkins (1969) tells us that for Lignac there can be no question that there is this internal aspect, an 'I', a self; he claims

...that Descartes was mistaken in his dictum 'Je pense, donc je suis' since all that he needed to say was 'Je'. The use of the first person pronoun assumes all that is supposedly proved by the forthcoming statement.

(Perkins, 1969, p. 50)

Harre defines this 'self' as '... the still centre of experience, that to which conscious states of all kinds are ascribed' (1987, p.99). He goes on to expand by explaining that the task of the self is to link with memory, perception and agency, while the person aspect of human beings is what is involved in the practical and interactive aspect of being.

MacMurray (1969) does not completely agree with this description of the self; he maintains that the self is not only the reflective aspect of one's being but that this cannot be abstracted from the acting and active part of an individual. He says,

The Self that reflects and the Self that acts is the same Self; action and thought are constructed modes of its activity. But it does not follow that they have an equal status in the being of the Self. In thinking the mind alone is active. In acting the body indeed is active, but also the mind. Action is not blind. When we turn from reflection to action we do not turn from consciousness to unconsciousness. When we act, sense perception and judgement are in continuous activity, along with physical movement.

(MacMurray, 1969, p. 86)

This is certainly tied to the earlier discussion of personhood and morality, as the self may be seen as the 'machine' or device within us which 'processes' or considers our options in terms of actions linked to what we consider to be right or wrong in relation to our moral code and the code of the moral majority. It is in this sense that the self, through the I, interacts with the external world but the self is placed internally in its reflective mode. Indeed, Perkins, in her study of the *Concept of Self in the French Enlightenment* understands Descartes as placing the self in the position of understanding the world around it: 'The whole structure of Descartes' system depends on the *Cogito* functioning in two directions:

one inwardly and the other outwardly ... Without the awareness of the self, a human being would not be able to have any knowledge at all' (1969, p. 14).

So, it may be argued, the self gives us knowledge of an outside world; it aids our understanding and gives some meaning to what is external to our mental existence. Perkins, commenting on d'Alembert, suggests that in his writings '... we have a separation of the two functions of the self, the *I* as initiator and ultimate being and the *me* as a collection of sensations' (*ibid.*, p. 45). Perkins claims that

> Energy is at the very heart of the self; it is in movement just as the rest of the universe is, and we find that at the centre of Diderot's concept of the self not a still quiet pool but a bubbling fountain.
>
> (*ibid.*, p. 127)

The self is an *active* agent, acting on behalf of the I, the 'ultimate being'; acting in the sense that it is reflecting and influencing the behaviour of the individual. Schrag (1997), in his study of the self, states that

> ... knowledge of a self is as much the rendering of an account, the telling of a story, as it is the discernment of perceptual profiles – and indeed it is the telling of a story in which the self is announced as at once the actor and receiver of action.
>
> (Schrag, 1997, p. 1)

The self has the responsibility of existing in an external material world without a physical presence of its own. The self is that acting, processing and understanding entity that helps to shape the I while, at the same, it receives information from the external world and the other individuals with selves that inhabit it. As Rousseau suggests, 'It is only by movement that we learn the difference between self and not self' (1948, p. 31); we must interact with the external in order to have some comprehension of the internal, the self.

There is, however, a problem with the language involved in

discussing oneself – or one's self. To talk of *my* self is to discuss the self as a possession, a thing; it exists in the third-person. *I*, however, exists in the first-person. So, the self, the it, belongs to the I. So, in order to know the I, one must know the self; the self goes towards making the I what it is. Taylor speaks of a 'radically reflexive' stance; he states that 'The stance becomes radical when what matters to us is the adoption of the first-person standpoint' (1989, p. 130). He continues,

> Radical reflexivity brings to the fore a kind of presence to oneself which is inseparable from one's being the agent of experience, something to which access by its very nature is asymmetrical: there is a crucial difference between the way I experience my activity, thought, and feeling, and the way that you or anyone else does. This is what makes me a being that can speak of itself in the first person.
>
> (*ibid.*, p. 131)

This is what entitles me to talk about I. It seems, therefore, that experience and interaction have prime roles in shaping the self that in turn shapes the I.

Rousseau appears, during one of his Reveries, also to posit the idea that selves do not exist in isolation, that their existence and their shaping of the I necessarily have a social dimension. He asks 'But I, detached from them and from everything, what am I?' (1979, p. 1). So, if we follow Rousseau's line, the I, which is shaped somehow by the self, is in turn formed with its relationship to the external world. The experience we have of interacting with this external environment and those other beings – or selves – in that environment helps us understand – or even *become* what we are. In fact, if we recall the previous chapter and the discussion of being and becoming, we should rather talk in terms of the external environment and other selves working in conjunction with one's own individual self to help us not *become* but *be*. One cannot talk of one's self as becoming since one would then never *be* anything; existence, or identity, would in some sense always be transient and could never be pinpointed. Thus, by always being in a state of becoming we would have an additional reason to lose the notion of child. Not only in terms of personhood is the notion of child treated as one of becoming, if we are to argue that one's self is always becoming, then the child suffers the double blow of being overlooked also in relation to its very identity. This is perhaps an issue that would not have existed prior to the seventeenth century when the notion of childhood was, some would argue, invented; however, with these two facets of one's identity with which to contend, children are most certainly perceived differently to adults. MacIntyre (1999) goes back in history to consider the way in which individuals were understood:

> ...in much of the ancient and medieval worlds, as in many other premodern societies, the individual is identified and constituted in and through certain of his or her roles, those roles which bind the individual to the communities in and through which alone specifically human goods are to be attained, I confront the world as a member of this family, this household, this clan, this tribe, this city, this nation, this kingdom. There is no 'I' apart from these.
>
> (MacIntyre, 1999, p. 172)

And as MacIntyre suggests that we cannot separate ourselves from society and its constituent parts to which we are attached or upon which we depend, he sees these role structures and ascriptions as inextricably linked to our concept of self; 'The individual carries his communal roles with him as part of the definition of his self' (*ibid.*, p. 173). We should also bear in mind here that children may have the role of person. So, if one has the ascription person, then this will influence the self, as person is ultimately a description of some aspect of one's self – one's identity – and in being persons we are social beings and cannot escape this fact.

The Moral Self

Additionally, while being social animals, we must also exist as moral creatures since living among others requires us to act in certain ways. Taylor (1989) recognizes this when he says that

... being a self is inseparable from existing in a space of moral issues to do with identity and how we ought to be. It is being able to find one's standpoint in this space, being able to occupy, to *be* a perspective in it.

(Taylor, 1989, p. 112)

Taylor's statement should be taken further; the ideas of the self may even be omitted in order to say that 'What we are constantly losing from sight here is that *being* is inseparable from existing in a space of moral issues ...' I would, however, agree with Taylor when he suggests that 'Selfhood and the good, or in another way, selfhood and morality, turn out to be inextricably intertwined themes' (*ibid.*, p. 3), since we exist in a moral world with other selves where moral issues arise. Again, we cannot abstract children from this moral world. By virtue of their being and their being in a social setting – no matter how disenfranchised or powerless they may be – children too exist in 'a space of moral issues'. It suits adult sensibilities and power structures that children should not be acknowledged as having any kind of moral sense or perspective; however, this is not the case. It was suggested earlier that we are born with a con-science, born with the ability to discern right from wrong and good from bad and that our moral codes are socialized and moulded into the accepted codes for existing in a particular society. Even although this may be the case, children are not then absented from the moral world and have moral decisions or interactions that they must make. For instance, they will choose with whom to be friends, they must decide what games to play or how they will interact with other individuals. In other words, they will often be offered choices and they must elect which to take, and bearing in mind that actions are invariably moral, they are making moral choices. So, no matter how small a choice is seen to be in terms of the adult determined morality, children do make moral choices, they do have opinions on what they prefer or think about their society in general and they must be allowed this if we are to maintain their per-sonhood in that they be treated as ends in themselves and not in terms of becoming, which in turn allows that their morality and their selfhood are inextricably linked like adult human beings, as Taylor suggested.

We need that external force of other individuals and experiences
to help us *be*; Taylor suggests that 'One is only a self among other
selves. A self can never be described without reference to those who
surround it' (*ibid.*, p. 35). Yet, Taylor appears to be inconsistent
here as he seems to suggest that 'one' *is* a self, and then he goes on
to say that 'I can only know myself through the history of my
maturations and regressions, overcomings and defeats' (*ibid.*, p. 50).
At one time he is implying that 'one' *is* one's self – the two are
interchangeable names for the same thing – but this second
statement demonstrates that *I* can know my *self*. Again, there is
this third-person self that is, as Taylor agrees, created through one's
life experiences. Yet, if this were the case, that one's self is created
by one's life experiences in the external world, one would have to
complete a whole lifetime in order to have formed some complete
self to shape the 'I'. Perkins states that the self '. . . is created as one
goes along in life and only posterity will be able to judge the whole
self of the individual' (1969, p. 130). We are not, however, discussing the *judgement* of the self, for what would this mean? This
implies some form of moral adjudication; has Individual X a good
self, that is, has he/she led a good life by the parameters set out by
the prevailing moral code? What is of more direct importance here
is that it should be asserted that the self cannot be defined at the
end of a lifetime, for then one would never have had a self, and by
the time it was able to be reflected upon in its complete state there
would be no point in its existence in the first – or rather final –
place as the individual who possesses the self will have expired as
will his/her existence in the moral world and so the self would have
no discernible function. What we can say is that the self is constantly changing in its different environments at different points in
the life of a human being as it encounters new experiences which
will impact upon how that individual interacts and relates with
those others in its social and moral world.

The Continuous Self

Further, and to pick up on the issue of completing one's life in order to create one's identity, one should bear in mind that as the self changes in its perspective of the world, the I or me is also evolving as it is being formed by the self. Lewis (1976) uses the example of Methuselah to explain the idea that we might be a composite series of selves. At age 323 Methuselah will not remember everything he did at 75 years of age and even less so at 12, and similarly, by the time he reaches 900 he will not recall everything he did at 323. Perry talks about '... person-stages ... a set of simultaneous experiences all of which belong to one person' (1975, p. 15), which may help us to understand Lewis' Methuselah example that we are a composite of selves that have existed at different times in our lives but each event or thought or experience will influence the individual we are at a particular point in time. Parfit (1976), in his discussion of Lewis, does not see the need to link the I now with the I in the future:

> When we ask if it is in *my* self-interest to save for my old age, we can ignore the R-relatedness [continuity and connectedness] of my old age to me now, for we are not asking about the interests of *me now*.
>
> (Parfit, 1976, p. 99)

Parfit's point is flawed – he fails to acknowledge that in talking about *me* at whatever time, he is referring to the same individual, so the R-relatedness cannot be ignored or overlooked. My interests in the future bear heavily on my interests now, although I may not always recognize what this implies in terms of practical living, for example saving money or changing job. Rorty (1976b) highlights our interest in someone's being the same person (with the same moral implications suggested earlier) and why we see it as important:

> ... we need to know whom to reward and whom to punish for actions performed when 'they' were acknowledgedly different in some respects from the present population ... we want to know what traits remain

constant so that we can know what we can expect from the persons around us. We assign crucial responsibilities to individuals, assume important continuing relations to them in the belief that certain of their traits are relatively constant or predictable.

(Rorty, 1976b, p. 4)

She goes on to explain why it is important on a personal level, and this refutes Parfit's dismissal of R-relatedness earlier:

And for ourselves, we are interested in our own identity because we make choices that will affect our futures: we set in motion a train of actions whose consequences involve 'our' well-being, without knowing whether we shall have, in the future, the desires and beliefs that now direct our planning.

(*ibid.*, p. 4)

Indeed, we cannot know about our future – we cannot even be sure that we have one – but our actions and the decisions we make and interactions we have assume that we have one. We build on our previous experiences or believe we have had previous experiences because of where we are *now*. For example, I can buy a pair of shoes today because I am sure that for the whole of last month I worked and was paid for my efforts. This does not simply mean that I buy the shoes today for today, for now; in making such a purchase I am working under the assumption that there will be another time when I can wear the shoes, another time in the future, and I can reasonably expect this to be the case as it has worked before on every previous occasion that I have bought shoes – for there is a vast collection at the bottom of my wardrobe. Similarly, in the way we behave towards children there is an implied future. If there were no such future we would not consider schooling such an important issue, we would not socialize children into the accepted and acceptable codes by which our society functions. In other words, we would not create the period of time known as childhood and then subvert it for the creation of the future adult society if we were not convinced of our futures.

The notion of a constant I or self with these transient experiences is also held by Reid. In his consideration of personal identity, Reid (1975) holds that

> My personal identity, therefore implies the continued existence of that indivisible thing which I call *myself*. Whatever this self may be, it is something which thinks, and deliberates, and resolves, and acts, and suffers. My thoughts, and actions, and feelings, change every moment; they have no continued, but a successive existence; but that *self* or *I*, to which they belong, is permanent, and has the same relation to all the succeeding thoughts, actions and feelings which I call mine.
>
> (Reid, 1975, p. 109)

It may be held, then, that identity implies some kind of continued existence; Reid is one proponent of this view:

> I see evidently that identity supposes an uninterrupted continuance of existence. That which has ceased to exist cannot be the same with that which afterwards begins to exist; for this would be to suppose a being to exist after I ceased to exist, and to have had existence before it was produced, which are manifest contradictions. Continued uninterrupted existence is therefore necessarily implied in identity.
>
> (*ibid.*, p. 108)

So, in order for a tree to have an identity, it must have had continued, uninterrupted existence, and likewise, for a human to have an identity it must equally have existed without stopping. A cessation of consciousness such as a sound sleep is not a limit on existence; death, it would seem, would stop a continued existence. Yet how can one be sure of one's uninterrupted existence? In his *Essay Concerning Human Understanding* Locke (1976) states that

> ...if two or more actions be joined together in the same mass, every one of those atoms will be the same ...; and whilst they exist united together, the mass, consisting of the same atoms, must be the same mass, or the same body, let the parts be never so differently jumbled; but if one of these atoms be taken away, or a new one added, it is no

longer the same body. In the state of living creatures, their identity depends not on a mass of the same particles but on something else.

(Locke, 1976, p. 158)

This is exactly how physical things exist in the universe, be those things trees, humans, rivers or hippos; indeed Hume says that 'An infant becomes a man, and is sometimes fat, sometimes lean, without any change in his identity' (1975, p. 307). Indeed, as a baby matures physically its mass will change in that various particles will be added such as teeth and hair and as the individual gets older some will be lost, such as teeth and hair, yet the individual is still the same entity. So what is it about us that changes as far as particles are concerned, but remains constant regarding our identity?

Identity

While our physical characteristics may alter from year to year, or indeed from day to day, there is something about *me* that remains the same. I could have blonde hair today, and red hair and a broken leg tomorrow, but *I* is still the same; I still know myself as would others that have been of my acquaintance. In fact, I look nothing like I did as a newborn baby, but I know that I am myself – but there are others who will verify this. My parents and relatives have been constants – their behaviour towards me and their recognition of my physical appearance confirms *I* remain the same. In fact, had I been in a horrific accident, lost my memory and been disfigured I would still have awoken and known I was me – for who else could I be? Rousseau uses the faculty of memory as an indicator of selfhood; he believes that memory is the criterion for delineating one's identity: 'What I do know is this, that my personal identity depends upon memory, and that to be indeed the same self I must remember that I have existed' (1948, p. 246). Reid, however, goes a step further: 'There can be no memory of what is past without the conviction that we existed at the time remembered' (1969, p. 338). Reid's *conviction* is more than a memory, it implies that *I* must have existed at a certain point and remember that I did in fact carry out the specific action or have the specific experience at that specific point in time. This is similar to what was discussed earlier in the chapter about our functioning in terms of a future in light of what we know about our past. However, problems arise when we falsely recall something or when we cannot or do not recall something; surely we do not lose the identity we possess. No, for if one does not lose one's identity when one has amnesia as a result of the car accident, then one cannot hold that memory itself is a necessary condition of identity.

Quinton (1975) suggests that our physical appearance is not what defines our identity either; he says that

> In our general relations with other human beings their bodies for the most part are intrinsically unimportant. We use them as convenient recognition devices enabling us to locate without difficulty the persisting character and memory complexes in which we are interested, which we love or like.
>
> (Quinton, 1975, p. 64)

So, we acknowledge that there are other beings with which we interact for a variety of purposes, yet we equally would maintain that there is something – other than physical space – that makes us separate and distinct from those of our fellow species. Our identity, then, must be extremely close in its liaison with our 'I'. In fact, when we talk of me or I, we talk of our identity – we are describing what one actually *is*, our mode of being; we are not talking about the identity *of* our 'I' – our identity *is* the 'I'. We break away from the third-person perspective when discussing our identity. The self belongs to the I/identity, it works for the 'I' and helps shape it. MacMurray sees the self as the thing that separates the 'you' from the 'I'. He posits that ' "The Self" is identical in all thinking beings; or to put it otherwise, we are identical in so far as we are rational' (1970, p. 19). Gillett (1987) also acknowledges this rational aspect of an individual's being, or his/her identity:

I have no experience or 'impression' or 'intuition' of an 'inner me', but I can be sure, nevertheless, that there *is* an essential unity in all my thought. My thought, to be coherent, must be the thought of a persistent rational being.

(Gillett, 1987, p. 83)

If we consider one of our initial questions of what it is that separates us from the other animals we inhabit the planet with, we have seen that the attribution of personhood is one such aspect with its expected patterns of behaviour and code acceptance; also there is our notion of self that can be considered at different times in different contexts and experiences; and now there is the suggestion that rationality and the ability to reason may be another. Locke (1976) is a proponent of the view that our ability to reason sets us apart from the 'beasts'. We have the faculty and facility to think; it is, he says, what we are:

...a thinking intelligent being that has reason and reflection and can consider itself as itself, the same thinking thing in different times and places; which it does only by that consciousness which is inseparable from thinking and, as it seems to me, essential to it: it being impossible for anyone to perceive without perceiving that he does perceive.

(Locke, 1976, p. 162)

The reasoning capacity, though, is not all that we, as humans, are. Locke maintains that we can reflect also; we can reflect and respond to the reasoning of others. He also maintains that we have consciousness. Locke would suggest personal identity is formed by consciousness:

For if we take wholly away all consciousness of our actions and sensations, especially of pleasure and pain, and the concernment that accompanies it, it will be hard to know wherein to place personal identity.

(*ibid.*, p. 38)

Reid (1969) disagrees; he states that

Identity can only be affirmed of things which have a continued existence. Consciousness, and every kind of thought, is transient and momentary, and has no continued existence; and therefore, if personal identity consisted in consciousness, it would certainly follow, that no man is the same person any two moments of his life.

(Reid, 1969, p. 360)

He goes on to state that if consciousness were in fact responsible for the creation of our personal identity, we would cease to exist when unconscious, such as in a sound sleep. All things, for Locke, are put in a pot of attributes that make us something more than human. He holds that 'Consciousness is the perception of what passes in a man's own mind' (Locke, 1976, p. 42). Consciousness, one might say, is the awareness of the world around us – it perceives the external world in which we function and the self, in its turn, makes sense of the perceptions. However, it could be argued that the consciousness, which will in turn work with the self in order to comprehend the perceptions, also has an element of influence if one allows it the facility to select what it perceives or elect what to be aware of. One cannot perceive that one perceives or would have difficulty being aware that one is aware. No, it is posited that our awareness is a passive mover in the life of I. Consciousness is an example of the animal impulses referred to in Chapter 1, which Chrysippus talked of. This is one of the facets of being human that we share with the other animals. Wild and domestic animals are aware of their surroundings in terms of spatial awareness, content of environment, and the like. Equally, they are conscious of their own society and its constituent parts, be that a cat with its garden territory or a wolf with its territory in the wilderness. They share this sense with humans; they know their area and recognize a stranger in their midst. It is simply that for humans society is a larger unit and strangers are not necessarily regarded with suspicion, but that has more to do with our notion of society and other individuals within it; a notion that has moved away from the awareness of the animals to the rational aspect possessed by human beings. This consciousness is a capacity that we are born with – we are born aware of our surroundings and wider environment. It is the self which processes these perceptions received by the senses, but it is our reason that, according to Locke, gives us more than an awareness. It may be argued that very young babies and infants lack the consciousness or awareness Locke talks about, however, it may be that these very young, unsocialized individuals are more animal in nature and have not yet learned the 'appropriate' or expected forms of behaviour. After all, when we watch wildlife footage, young lion or bear cubs are inquisitive and adventurous; they have not yet learned to be cautious of certain other creatures or to avoid certain types of objects. Infant human beings are the same in this regard; they have not learned to distrust strangers and will try to do things or touch objects that they have not yet learned may cause harm. Nonetheless, all animals do have some level of consciousness or awareness of their environment and surroundings, and all want to examine them further. It is human children, however, that inquire in a certain way, a way which involves reason and reflection, asking questions and posing hypotheses. In essence, human infants are rational, or at least have the potential to be rational, in a way which other animals do not. This rationality is something that is also necessary in our social context and this social context brings us into direct contact with other individuals, and by virtue of our interaction we function by employing our moral codes. Bearing in mind that it was suggested that our morality could not be extracted from our social context and vice versa, we can only function in our relations with others, whatever their age or status, in a moral manner and we need to be able to reason about these moral actions. Mayo suggests that moral principles are a function of reason and 'Only a rational being can have principles, though non-rational beings can have feelings and even express them' (1986, p. 55).

Here we have an obvious problem, as not every human being is considered a rational, reasoning or reflective human individual. Without even considering the issue of those individuals suffering from mental illness or those in a vegetative state, there are others in our society who are perceived of as lacking this reasoning faculty, this step beyond consciousness, this ability to be rational – children. The issue of children as rational agents will be discussed later in the book. It should also be noted that in talking of an individual having the *potential* to be rational or to reason, one is not meaning in the sense of becoming and developing as discussed in Chapter 1, but rather, that *all* humans have this potential, this capacity and not all use it fully, if at all.

Conclusions

In this chapter it has been argued that in some respects human beings are set apart and distinct from the other animals on the planet. It has been suggested that humans have a reflexive perspective, they have a self, an internal processor which, while located internally, reflects upon the external world in order to create some understanding and in turn help to shape the I or identity of an individual. This self exists only among other selves. Where there are other selves there is a 'space of moral issues' and it is this which the self reflects upon. It cannot be the case that one can only possess a self in its entirety at the end of one's lifetime as we would continually be in a state of becoming. In behaving towards others as becomings, then, we negate our definition of personhood as one where we treat others as ends in themselves and not simply as a means to an end. While there is this sense that we are not becomings, that we actually *are* and *are* in the now, we cannot neglect that there is some continuity and connectedness in our identity. We must act in a way that assumes and presumes we have had a past and will have a future, as this is crucial, not merely for our functioning in a moral society, but also it is vital in our consideration of the child. Children are a part of the moral spaces we humans inhabit and they cannot be dismissed as *becoming* adults. Certainly the consciousness that the 'beasts' have is shared by humans, but humans have a reasoning and reflecting capacity that is not evident in other animals. And as children exist in our moral society, they too must be acknowledged as having the capacity and ability to reason. This reasoning about the moral world around us goes some way to forming our identities and it is the self which aids in the process. While children are not considered as dogs or hippos in many respects, this reasoning ability is one aspect where they are often treated on a par with domestic pets and wild animals. We should look now at how children have been viewed in and by society in the past in order to give us a clearer notion of how we treat children now, why we treat them in these ways and how we may behave towards them in the future. Let us briefly consider the history of children and their role in society until this point in time.

3

From Where Did Children Come?

In this chapter the notion of child and childhood will be considered in more recognized or familiar ways; the topics will be reviewed from historical and sociological perspectives. In order that we may judge how we have come to view children in the ways we do, then it is important we reflect upon how we got here. Also, in order that we can determine how children should be treated now and in the future we must consider the past. Gittins highlights that 'Approaches to studying the history of childhood vary quite considerably' (2004, p. 25) and this study is further influenced by postmodern theory. It should be noted that this chapter is not intended as a full history of the topic of childhood, but that the discussion within this chapter is intended to provide a context for the bigger *philosophical* considerations surrounding it.

'Childhood, in the strict etymological sense, is the age when the man to be cannot yet speak (from the Latin *in-fans*, not speaking)' (Durkheim, 1982, p. 146). While Durkheim is keen to stress the etymological root of the word *childhood*, there is much debate and confusion over its meaning as a *concept*. For our purposes here, the concept *childhood* shall stand by Archard's (1993) definition, that childhood

> ... is an abstract noun which denotes the state of being or the stage at which one is a child. Its use dictates a certain formal and sophisticated grasp of what and when it is to be a child, one that abstracts from the particulars of individual children.... A society could have an

'awareness' of the 'particular nature' of *children* without possessing a *concept* of childhood.

(Archard, 1993, p. 17)

Gittins (2004) supports the notion of 'child' and 'childhood' as being of a different order when she says that

> 'Child' therefore defines not just psychological immaturity but also connotes dependency, powerlessness and inferiority. Child*hood*, however, focuses more on the general state of being a child, does not refer to an individual child and suggests the existence of a distinct, separate and fundamentally different social group or category.

(Gittins, 2004, p. 27)

A New Notion

Perhaps the first to discuss the issue of children and childhood as a subject worthy of serious consideration was Philippe Ariès. While he offers no definition of childhood, he holds that prior to the seventeenth century there was no such thing as childhood as a separate stage. Cunningham agrees in his discussion on the eighteenth century that 'Some people began to see childhood as a preparation for something else, whether adulthood or heaven, but as a stage of life to be valued in its own right' (1995, p. 61). There is a problem here, that when we start to set new categories and define individuals differently, we must then treat them and behave towards them in a different way. In this instance the world of people became split, if we are to follow Ariès, into the world of adults and the world of children; we cannot define one without reference to the other. Indeed, Archard (1993) maintains that

> The *concept* of childhood requires that children be distinguishable from adults in respect of some unspecified set of attributes. A *conception* of childhood is a specification of those attributes. In simple terms to have a concept of 'childhood' is to recognise that children differ

interestingly from adults; to have a conception of childhood is to have a view of what those interesting differences are...

(Archard, 1993, p. 22)

Indeed, Cunningham's point may be the case *historically*, but Jenks (1996), while supporting Archard, sums up the problem needing to be addressed when he says that the child

... cannot be imagined except in relation to a conception of the adult, but essentially it becomes impossible to generate a well-defined sense of adult, and indeed adult society, without first positing the child.

(Jenks, 1996, p. 3)

This is what will be considered in this chapter, the deceptively simple question: 'What *is* a child?'

Matthews agrees that the issue deserves some consideration: '... the concept of childhood is philosophically problematic in that genuine philosophical difficulties stand in the way of saying just what *kind* of difference the difference between children and adult human beings is' (1994, p. 8). Sociologically, historically, psychologically and educationally there is an abundance of material written about children and childhood. Even in our every day discourse we speak in such a way that assumes there is some recognized definition of the term 'child' – but there is not. Archard maintains that 'Locke exemplifies a philosophical tradition of understanding children in a mixture of epistemological, educational and political terms. The Problem,' he sees – and I agree – 'is how these various ways of thinking about children may consistently be combined one with another' (1998, p. 95). Not only must we consider what children actually are, but also we must take stock of how these perceptions influence behaviour in our society towards children and the part they are expected to play.

One would naturally acknowledge that a child is in the first place a human being, by virtue of the fact that we are conceived and brought into the world by 'adult' parents, parents who, as human beings themselves, reproduce their own species. Jenks poses that 'In the everyday world the category of childhood is a totalizing concept, it concretely describes a community that at some time has everybody as its member' (1996, p. 6). In effect, we have all been – and still are – children, simply as a consequence of having parents. Jenks continues that childhood '. . . is the only truly common experience of being human, infant mortality is no disqualification' (*ibid.*, p. 6). We have all had experience, whatever that may mean, of being young in years and small in stature. And while we all begin life as a human being, the child '. . . is always in transition, and most obviously with respect to size' (Matthews, 1994, p. 23). However, we are not destined, in the main, to remain diminutive in size; in *Emile* Rousseau points out that '. . . speaking generally, man is not meant to remain a child. He leaves childhood behind him at the time ordained by nature; and this critical moment, short enough in itself, has far reaching consequences' (1948, p. 172). Archard agrees that this is the case: 'Since childhood is a developmental process whose end is adulthood, children would seem to be imperfect, incomplete versions of their adult selves' (1998, p. 86). They, children, are given the message that Matthews finds 'unmistakable', that 'You are not (yet) a full member of society' (1994, p. 22) – and this is to what one must aspire. So, while it is clear that at birth children are human beings, they appear to lack something adult human beings possess.

This is a strange notion, for – as appears to have been the case – this is not how things always were. Ariès (1996) sets the tone for the place of the concept of child and childhood in our present society. He says,

> We are so accustomed now to thinking of childhood as essential to any notion of our own personal history, and identity, it is difficult to remember that childhood itself – as both an ordinary preoccupation, and an academic subject worthy of study – has a history.
>
> (Ariès, 1996, p. 5)

Again, let it be clearly stated that the concept of childhood is not at issue here; childhood is that period of time in one's life when one is a child, and it is to this concept, *child*, that we should address ourselves.

As stated earlier in this chapter, Ariès holds that childhood did not exist prior to the seventeenth century. Becker (1998) offers an alternative viewpoint, he claims that

> There is evidence, however, that the Stoics paid *better* attention than their rivals did to observing, describing and making theoretical use of the behavior of children, because they gave us a subtle and powerful *developmental* psychology – an account that begins with acute observations of the behavior of infants and very young children.
>
> (Becker, 1998, p. 45)

Early Children

For the Stoics, according to Becker, the developmental process from child to adult human being was very clear:

> ...children grow and mature ... Newborns have a small array of crude, primal impulses and very limited powers. Infants and children increase in size and physical strength; their powers of locomotion and perception increase; they accumulate memories from a wider and wider range of experience; new powers (notably language) and new impulses (notably reproduction) are added to their repertoires as they ripen into adolescence and adulthood – and some are subtracted as adults move through middle and old age; children acquire useful habits of inquiry, inference and conduct, which they refine through trial and error; they generalize, hypothesize, observe outcomes, and acquire a more or less theoretical understanding of things, and eventually they may come to see that practical wisdom requires them to be just, courageous, temperate, benevolent – in a word, virtuous.
>
> (*ibid.*, p. 50)

There is much here of interest, and some of the points will be discussed later, however, this serves, initially, to demonstrate that certainly prior to the seventeenth and eighteenth centuries there *were* those interested in considering child human beings as something distinct from adult human beings. Certainly, according to Cunningham, 'Neither Greek nor Latin had any equivalent to the word "baby" but each had a variety of words signifying child, but rarely restricted to that' (1995, p. 23). Further, Cunningham adds, that in classical Athens, 'If children who died were mourned, it was because they were perceived to have lived to no purpose, not having reached adulthood. Childhood itself cannot be praised, thought Cicero, only its potential' (*ibid.*, p. 26). This certainly seems to concur with Matthews' earlier point that has remained true, it would seem, from the time of Cicero and the Ancients until now, that children are not fully part of society, there is something which sets or keeps them apart. Children, women and slaves were kept in society's margins; according to Cunningham it would seem that

> Part of this marginality [for children] stemmed from the likelihood that they may die before reaching adulthood and becoming part of society; certainly if they died very young they were subject to quite different burial customs from older people, being buried inside the city walls rather than outside, sometimes in the foundations of buildings, and at night.
>
> (*ibid.*, p. 25)

So, it would appear, that while children were, in classical times, not equal to adults, the Stoics were possibly the first to consider the question of what a child *is*, or at least to pay some serious attention to what constitutes, or forms, an adult. The notion of potentiality seems to be the key to those thinkers of ancient times. The idea of potentiality was not limited to the ancients however; it is still very much part of the perspective which colours society today and will be discussed further, later in this book.

Medieval Children

In the Middle Ages children were not cut off from adult society in the sense that they mingled freely with their older neighbours. Ariès claims that in the Romanesque world, '... right up to the thirteenth century, there are no children characterized [in art and architecture] by a special expression but only men on a reduced scale' (1996, p. 32). He continues that when we get further into the thirteenth century '. . . a few types of children are to be found which appear to be a little closer to the modern concept of childhood' (*ibid.*, p. 32). The model child depicted in art around this time was the Infant Jesus. Tucker takes up this point, that 'With the Christ Child as the model, how could children be anything but innocent? They had no sexual desire; they did not know evil in adult ways' (1995, p. 231). Cunningham would disagree with Ariès and Tucker in their interpretation of using the image of the painting of Jesus as a baby as a guide to understanding how children were regarded; he maintains that it '. . . tells us about changes in theology, not attitudes to childhood' (1995, p. 32).

Certainly in the Middle Ages, children, even before the age of seven, were not kept out of adult society and company. Ariès (1996) uses medieval art as a tool to understanding the role played by children in those times. He states that

> These subject paintings were not as a general rule devoted to the exclusive portrayal of childhood, but in a great many cases there were children among the characters depicted, both principal and secondary. And this suggests the idea, first that children mingled with adults in everyday life, and any gathering for the purpose of work, relaxation or sport brought together both children and adults; and secondly, that painters were particularly fond of depicting childhood for its graceful or picturesque qualities.
>
> (Ariès, 1996, p. 36)

There was little, other than size, that differentiated a child from an adult in the Middle Ages. Ariès points out

> The marked indifference shown until the thirteenth century – except where the infant Virgin was concerned – to the special characteristics of childhood does not appear simply in the world of pictures: the dress of the period shows to what extent, in the circumstances of real life, childhood was distinguished from manhood as soon as the baby abandoned his swaddling-band – he was dressed just like the other men and women in his class.
>
> (*ibid.*, p. 48)

Only class was highlighted in an individual's attire, '... the Middle Ages dressed every age indiscriminately, taking care only to maintain the visible vestiary signs of the differences in the social hierarchy. Nothing in medieval dress distinguished the child from the adult' (*ibid.*, p. 48). Even in the educational settings of schools and colleges, says Ariès, children were placed with older counterparts; 'As soon as he started going to school, the child immediately entered the world of adults. This ... was one of the most characteristic features of medieval society and one of the most enduring too' (*ibid.*, p. 150). In the fourteenth and fifteenth centuries, however, it should be remembered that a boy between the ages of 13 and 15 was already considered to be a fully-grown man, and as Ariès holds, '... shared in the life of his elders, without causing any surprise' (*ibid.*, p. 159). Cunningham (1995) warns us that

> There is a danger that 'medieval childhood', perhaps stretching back by inference prior to the twelfth century, and certainly covering the whole of Europe, will be set up as something which can be compared and contrasted with childhood in other eras, with the nuances, ambivalences and changes within the period being forgotten.
>
> (Cunningham, 1995, p. 38)

However, this must equally be true with respect to any time and culture, and therefore, one can only bear Cunningham's remarks in mind and attempt not to compare and contrast on an equal plain. Ariès (1996), in his study of childhood, states that

> ... although demographic conditions did not greatly change between the thirteenth and seventeenth centuries, and although child mortality remained at a very high level, a new sensibility granted these fragile, threatened creatures a characteristic which the world had hitherto failed to recognise in them: as if it were only then that the common conscience had discovered that the child's soul too was immortal. There can be no doubt that the importance accorded to the child's personality was linked with the growing influence of Christianity on life and manners.
>
> (Ariès, 1996, p. 41)

A Class Apart

Indeed, Postman affirms the point that in the Middle Ages 'There did not exist a rich content of formal behaviour for youth to learn' (1994, p. 16) and it is with the growing power of the Church that morality begins to be tempered and divided in terms of adult/child behaviour. In fact, it was owing to ecclesiastical opposition that child-marriage became less popular, as between the ninth and thirteenth centuries girls could marry at the minimum age of 12 and boys at the age of 14, with some being betrothed before then.

Postman holds that there was something beyond religion that accounts for the divide between children and adults in the fourteenth century – the 'knowledge gap' between those who could read and those who could not. 'Publication of books on paediatrics [1498 Paolo Bagallardo and 1544 Thomas Phaire] as well as those on manners is a strong indication that the concept of childhood had already begun to form, less than a century after the printing press' (*ibid.*, p. 29). This was a whole new world and could not be accessed by everyone. In fact, Postman argues, 'To be a fully functioning adult required one to go beyond custom and memory into worlds not previously known about or contemplated' (*ibid.*, p. 29). Previously, he maintains, there had been no need for a notion of childhood as everyone shared the same social world, the same environment, the same information and, therefore, the same intellectual world:

> From print onward, adulthood had to be earned. It became a symbolic, not a biological achievement. From print onward the young would have to *become* adults, and they would have to do it by learning to read, by entering the world of typography. And in order to accomplish that they would require education. Therefore, European civilization reinvented schools. And by so doing, it made childhood a necessity.
>
> (*ibid.*, p. 36)

With Ariès, we come to the end of the sixteenth century where children are now seen as separate entities, and as separate entities they must be distinguishable and this is done via a special costume for the younger members of society. Dress seems to be the most obvious manifestation of how children were and are regarded in society and culture; it gives us the first clue as to the way children are to be viewed on an initial encounter. This was primarily the case with social class:

> The children of the lower class ... went on wearing the same clothes as adults; they were never depicted in robes or false sleeves. [However] They kept up the old way of life which made no distinction between children and adults, in dress or in work or play.
>
> (Ariès, 1996, p.59)

It would therefore appear that those in the lower social classes were on an equal footing with children; perhaps this wasn't equality between ages, but a disparity in the apportioning of power within the community and a link to Postman's thesis regarding the advent of print. Ariès continues '... that in the early seventeenth century there was not such a strict division as there is today between children's games and those played by both children and adults. Young and old played the same games' (*ibid.*, p. 79).

There was, however, a change in attitude in the seventeenth and eighteenth centuries to the games played by both children and adults; children were forbidden to play games seen as 'evil' and were encouraged to play games that were 'good'. Ariès (1996) claims that this interest in and attitude towards such games was the advent of a new way of perceiving childhood; this is when children, their morality and the well-being of their eternal souls were seen in a way that was not much in evidence, if at all, in previous centuries.

Ariès claims that 'The idea began to spread that childhood was not a servile age, and that it did not deserve to be methodically humiliated' (*ibid.*, p. 252). Before this, according to King, philosophers like Hobbes believed childhood to be '... a period of servitude we would [today] call slavery' (1998, p. 65). He also viewed children – like wives and cattle – as objects of potential gain having '... rights over infants, children or any "feeble or subdued person" in much the same way we have dominion plain and simple over animals' (*ibid.*, p. 69). Indeed, Tucker lends weight to the suggestion that children were seen as workers, as individuals who contributed to the financial means of the family, or even 'stood on their own two feet'; 'In the lower reaches of society, children were not kept at home but apprenticed to learn a trade' (1995, p. 250). Tucker continues by suggesting that apprenticeship was so highly regarded that it was shaped by national policy, and that in 1536 begging children between the ages of five and 14 were collected within parishes and apprenticed to unskilled jobs. The promotion of child labour was not simply used as a means to contribute to the family, there were wider implications which Hendrick highlights: 'For most children [by the end of the eighteenth century] labouring was held to be a condition which would teach them numerous economic, social and moral principles' (1997, p. 39). Even until the 1780s children were still regarded on the same footing as some adults, since until that point '... children could be convicted for any more than two hundred crimes for which the penalty was hanging' (Postman, 1994, p. 53). There was a sea-change afoot, however, with the advent of Locke and Rousseau, voices like Hobbes' were to be heard less and less.

Archard (1998) suggests that

> Locke appears to insist that the child has needs and interests which should be recognized for what they are, and that a child should be reasoned with, not simply beaten or coerced into conformity with the rules of required behaviour.
>
> (Archard, 1998, p. 86)

For Locke, adulthood was not so much a chronological age, but rather a state of mind. While Archard is somewhat dissatisfied with Locke's arguments about children and their rationality, he feels that Locke makes a '... far more productive suggestion that what is different about the production of a child is that it is the bringing into being of a human life' (*ibid.*, p. 93). He goes on to point out that as a human being the child is equally entitled to certain rights. In fact, he goes a little further by stating that the child is in *possession* of these rights – he/she already owns them, which implies something more than entitlement. When Locke was writing we again see, in dress, the outward signs of the emergence of an acknowledgment that children were in some way different or separate from adults; Ariès (1996) tells us that

> In the seventeenth century ... the child, or at least the child of quality, whether noble or middle class, ceased to be dressed like the grown up. This is the essential point: henceforth he had an outfit reserved for his age group, which set him apart from the adults.
>
> (1996, p. 48)

It should be noted perhaps that this was not the case for girls, who as soon as they were out of swaddling clothes were dressed like little women. Perhaps it could be argued that boys were children and girls were not. There is perhaps no argument here, as we have already seen, in considering the view taken by Hobbes, that women were as cattle – objects to be owned – thus girls would be no different to calves, waiting their turn to be utilized in the market place of marriage and child production. Ariès holds that 'The evidence provided by dress bears out other indications furnished by the history of manners: boys were the first specialized children' (*ibid.*, p. 56). By 'specialized children' one would understand Ariès to mean the first time young human beings had been given a category into which they could be placed and belong, and society could then take account of their status or place in that culture. Cunningham points out that we should remember that in the seventeenth century children '... constituted a much larger proportion of the population than they do now, and would have been correspondingly visible – and audible' (1995, p. 100). By the mid-eighteenth century, he asserts, children had become a focus of attention,

> Framed by the writings of John Locke at its beginning and of the romantic poets at its end, and with the strident figure of Rousseau at centre stage, there seems in the eighteenth century to be a degree of sensitivity to childhood and to children lacking in previous centuries.
>
> (*ibid.*, p. 61)

Romantic Children

While Locke showed some recognition of the individuality of each child, Rousseau, in *Emile*, took further the idea of child-centredness. Rousseau asked us to consider childhood: '... is there anything so weak and wretched as a child, anything so utterly at the mercy of those about it, so dependent on their pity, their care, and their affection?' (1948, p. 52). It is to the education of this dependent being that Rousseau turns his attention, 'Since the mere choice of things shown him may make the child timid or brave, why should not his education begin before he can speak or understand?' (*ibid.*, p. 30). Rousseau held that our education, our learning, came from and through our experiences of nature, other human beings and things. He wanted a free and 'natural' education for Emile, his protégé; this meant that 'Rather than reform the education that comes from men, Rousseau's plan for Emile involves systematically replacing the education he receives from men with an education from things' (Simon, 1998, p. 105). Cunningham is of the opinion that while Rousseau held in common with other thinkers and writers the value of education in producing a 'good adult', '... his radicalism lay in thinking that the way to do this was to allow children to grow up in accordance with nature, and without the imposition upon them of moral rules and learning' (1995, p. 67).

As we moved into the nineteenth century, children and childhood were being championed by social reformers. Cunningham addresses this new consideration of children and the ways in which social reformers sought to provide for them, albeit with a view to their future production potential:

> Childhood was being seen as at least in part a time for play. Without it children would not develop the bodily strength necessary for a successful adulthood, and in the cotton factories they were not receiving it.
>
> (*ibid.*, p. 139)

Certainly, at the very beginning of the nineteenth century, at New

Lanark, near Glasgow, Robert Owen – the manager of the cotton mills and factories – initiated the first nursery school in the world and provided lessons for the older children of the mill town, not only in reading, writing and arithmetic, but the children were also given music and dancing lessons. This project was much admired and imitated throughout the world and spawned a new type of education for the working classes. For Ariès 'This evolution of the educational institution is bound up with a parallel evolution of the concepts of age and childhood' (1996, p. 169). The nineteenth century would see, in its new concept of education, more of a bent towards preparing the child for adult life in a more gradual and careful way. This, one must add, is the idealized picture; it cannot be forgotten that very often in practice, education or schooling was far from ideal in its approach to learning, teaching or, indeed, the children themselves.

A child in nineteenth-century Britain was beginning to be defined as one in need of protection, as a dependent being, one offered protection by law, and thus, the government of the day who – advised by the Royal Commission – set out an Act of Parliament to protect the child until the age of 14 '... when the body becomes more capable of enduring protracted labour ...' (Cunningham, 1995, p. 140). In fact, argues Cunningham, one must not get carried away with the notion that the State and its inhabitants were only concerned with the well-being of its children. He holds that

> Compulsory schooling was introduced simply or mainly to try to provide all children with an experience of childhood. It has to be understood in a context of state rivalry, and a worry about the effectiveness of the socialization of children in the reproduction of the social order.
>
> (*ibid.*, p. 159)

There was schooling in the seventeenth century which led to a shift in social status for some as schooling was seen as the opportunity to create a literate adult who could – and would – function at a certain level within society. 'School learning,' as Postman puts it, 'became identified with the special nature of childhood' (1994, p.

41). He maintains that the ability to read was what ultimately separated children from adults and that adults who could not read were often regarded as intellectually *childish*. Wintersberger (1994) also raises this point and stresses that one should not become too excited by the idea that there was a shift away from child labour and that the exploitation of children was completely over, rather,

> The alternative for the capitalistic abuse of children became school. But school for working-class children of the nineteenth century should not be idealized. It was usually a small and ugly room, with the children supervised by ignorant teachers and kept like animals.
>
> (Wintersberger, 1994, p. 216)

Cunningham (1995) continues by saying that to achieve and maintain the notion of happy childhoods

> ... childhood had to be sharply separated from adulthood, and its characteristics and needs had to be recognized. Childhood and adulthood, in this thinking, became almost opposites of one another. If adults worked, children should not work. If adults had to live in towns, children were entitled to contact with nature.
>
> (1995, p. 160)

A series of Factory Acts in Britain by the end of the nineteenth century finally took children out of the world of adult work and

> ... fixed in law a difference in the spheres of social action for children and adults. This difference in turn marked out the distinctiveness of the status positions 'child' and 'adult' in the life course: play became the prerogative of children and work that of adults.
>
> (James *et al.*, 1998, p. 90)

By the end of the nineteenth century these new rights were not so much seen as rights to protection and education, but rather as a right to childhood itself.

We are not so far removed from the latter part of the twentieth century, but it is nonetheless important to consider the way in which children have come to be regarded in relatively recent years.

In Purdy's discussion of Firestone, she highlights Firestone's thesis
'... that artificial differences have been constructed between
humans who are essentially similar. These are then held to be
morally relevant differences that justify hierarchical relationships'
(1998, p. 190). This appears to imply that Firestone would hold a
common perception of children with those prior to the seventeenth
century, that children should, indeed, not be segregated from the
'adult' world. Rawls would apparently disagree: Brennan *et al.*
discuss Rawls' sympathy '... for the people who are the least
advantaged in society and surely the children of the least advantaged adults are even more vulnerable than the other members of
their families' (1998, p. 203); he would almost certainly hold that
such children should be entitled to special, individual treatment
that does, in fact, set them apart from the 'adult' world. Cunningham (1995), though, who seems to inhabit a more 'realistic'
and less idealized world than Rawls perhaps does, describes what he
sees to have happened in the second half of the twentieth century:

> ... parental authority has declined, and children have demanded and
> received an earlier access to the adult world, they have not been
> willing to accept the attempt to prolong childhood to the late teenage
> years. In some ways this represents a return to the historical norm in
> which childhood did not extend beyond fourteen at the maximum.
>
> (Cunningham, 1995, p. 185)

This, like Firestone, appears to see a shift back to how Ariès
described the Middle Ages, when there were little or no fixed
boundaries separating childhood from adulthood. Cunningham,
though, qualifies his acceptance of the situation in previous centuries and its difference to the society we currently inhabit:

> The difference is that in earlier centuries at the age of fourteen a
> person was economically productive whereas in the late twentieth
> century he or she will have a minimum of two years and quite
> probably a further seven or more years of non-productivity.
>
> (*ibid.*, p. 185)

This is the state in which we find ourselves, historically and practically, but we must now consider these issues on a philosophical – yet still practical – level.

Conclusions

It was suggested at the beginning of this chapter that childhood was not what needed to be defined, but that this was the time in one's life when one was considered as being a child. It has been posited that in medieval times there was no such distinction between individuals no matter their age; all mingled together, shared the same jokes and enjoyed the same games. In fact, the divide could be viewed more in terms of class and social status rather than one of age. With the advent of print and thus an increasing 'knowledge gap' and a desire or need for schooling, younger members of society were separated and segregated more and more from the older members of their social group. Added to this were the new and more 'child-centred' approaches of Locke and Rousseau which moved further away from Hobbes' notion of children as chattels and objects to do one's bidding. Kennedy (2006) claims that

> Both also reinforced for modernity an image of the child as a rudimentary condition, raw material for the new man of reason, to be produced through a systematic, theoretically driven ... program of socialization. For both, as paradigmatic moderns, the child represents nature, an untamed wilderness to be shaped and transformed by method.
>
> (Kennedy, 2006, p.91)

Locke and Rousseau, in their writings, paved the way for a whole new way of treating children, one which is still felt today; the child was different, the child was special and the child was an innocent whose innocence should be protected. Kehily suggests that this 'Romantic discourse claimed that children embody a state of innocence, purity and natural goodness that is only contaminated on contact with the corrupt outside world' (2004b, p. 5). As Britain moved into the nineteenth century, Factory Acts were being legislated and again childhood became the preserve of play, purity and innocence. Only in the recent past has there been a shift again towards the medieval view of society. With the increase and improvement in technology the 'knowledge gap' is lessening. The division between what is for children and what is for adults – or rather the accessibility of the products – is becoming more blurred. Younger and younger individuals have more and more power in the purchasing environment and are dictating more and more what they want to buy or own – increasingly what is desired is what their older siblings, their parents or their role models from music, film and television have. This fuzzing of the line between child and adult is what we must consider in terms of children's roles in society and how they interact – or are permitted to interact – within it.

4

The Reasoning Child

Let us return to the issue we left in Chapter 2 before we reviewed how children have been and are perceived in society: we considered the idea of being a rational being. It was suggested that to be a rational being one was able to reason and reflect upon thoughts and actions and would equally be able to justify the thoughts or actions concerned. We should consider whether this applies to children. In this chapter we will briefly reflect upon Piaget's stage maturation theory and consider how this equates with the reasoning and philosophical skills children exhibit. Reference will be made to Lipman and Matthews, both of whom have worked in the realm of philosophy with children. The idea of a closing 'knowledge gap' will be considered in more detail, as will the role toys play in the socialization of children. It will be demonstrated that the notion of child is a social phenomenon and one that relies heavily on the propagation of the 'correct' moral codes into society through the very young. In the main it will be maintained that, for children, being able to reason is as much a part of their make-up as it is for the adults within society.

Children Thinking

In this regard Aristotle does not *wholly* separate children from adults; he suggests that '... children and animals are as capable of voluntary action as adult men; but they have not the same capacity for deliberate choice' (1955, p. 82). This sentiment is echoed time and time again by philosophers, psychologists, educationalists and people in general, believing children to be inferior to adults in their rationalizing and reasoning abilities. Perhaps the most prominent proponent in perpetrating and perpetuating the idea that children are not fully rational beings was Piaget; his influence is still felt today in our educational systems and in the way children are generally viewed and treated by society. Piaget devoted much of his professional life to theorizing about the intellectual development of children, conducting experiments and publishing his findings. He was '. . . interested in the child's conception of the world and thus in the child's conception of what thought is' (Matthews, 1980, p. 45). The technique employed by Piaget for charting the child's intellectual development was to outline three or four stages of progression that demonstrated some kind of grasp of a concept; attaining this, the child would then move to the next stage before progressing to the one after that and ultimately reaching the final stage having attained a successful mastery of the content of the previous three stages. In using this methodology Piaget was able to suggest that a child should reach a specified intellectual stage by a certain age. By looking for patterns in children's responses Piaget aimed to find a standard response which would demonstrate the ways in which children's thinking emerges. In fact, when Piaget encountered an unusual response that did not conform to the set criteria, it was dismissed by him. Piaget's research concerning the cognitive developmental stages of growth in children aims to find patterns of response that are the same in all cases that arise: 'The only way to draw a line between what is occasional and what is permanent in the curiosity of a child is to multiply the records in conditions as similar as possible' (1960, p. 163). As for those statements made by children that do not conform to Piaget's pattern, they are labelled as 'romancing'; the child is asking a question that is '. . . merely verbal, and indicates pure astonishment without calling for any answer' (*ibid.*, p. 164). One might suggest that, rather than discard or ignore the unusual response as it does not fit a predefined category, the unusual or nonconforming response is one where there is evidence of reflection and consideration. Piaget maintains that the child '. . . explores and experiments until he finds an answer that satisfies him, and he achieves equilibrium, at least for his current stage of development' (Pulaski, 1980, p. 12). This accusation could be levelled at Piaget himself since he will not accept the unusual in terms of questions or answers from children by considering them as mere 'romancing'. 'Romancing', for Piaget, is '... inventing an answer in which [one] does not really believe, or in which [one] believes merely by the force of saying it' (Matthews, 1980, p. 139) – he does not consider children as having the capability to reason and justify while also considering the views of others. Piaget appears to lack patience with the philosophical observations or comments of the child.

Several of the children's comments in Piaget's experiments are so glaringly philosophical that it is strange that he could fail to notice their significance. His research provided the following questions, all of which could be considered philosophically: 'Does it [a caterpillar] know it has got to die if it becomes a butterfly?; Why do the trees have leaves?; Do grown up people make mistakes?; Are there people who are wicked because they are hungry?'(Piaget, 1960). Rather than consider these questions and the responses he was given from a philosophical perspective, Piaget seems to be more concerned with trying to prove his hypothesis while disregarding anything that may disprove his initial claims. He asserts that

> The mind seeks to understand and to explain at all levels, but the vague, incoherent explanations of childhood are a far cry from the richness and flexibility of adult thought. It is the search for equilibrium, for answers that satisfy, which spurs the mind onto higher levels of thought.
>
> (Pulaski, 1980, p. 11)

There is a false assumption here that it is adult human beings that are capable of this 'higher level of thought', that they search deeper or ask more probing questions than the younger members of our society. If Piaget's tests and stage theory were to be applied to everyone, it would undoubtedly be seen that not everyone would always attain Piaget's fourth stage – even well into their adulthood.

One cannot put a label on thinking. In department stores signs indicate 'Children's Wear' – this part of the store is designed and set up to cater for clothing for children's smaller bodies, however, it does not disqualify smaller adults from purchasing clothes from this section. Similarly, book shops and libraries reference their sections with 'Adult Fiction' and 'Children's Fiction'; one does not necessarily negate the other – an adult can select from the 'Children's Fiction' section and a child can similarly select from the 'Adult Fiction' section. It would seem unlikely that labels could easily or realistically be attached to thinking – the idea of 'Adult Thinking' and 'Children's Thinking' would be hard, if not impossible, to distinguish. There are those who would consider certain thinking as being 'childish'; this is a particularly negative perspective, intended not as a compliment, but as a remonstration to an adult for his/her simplistic expression or idea. On the contrary, simplicity and clarity of expression is no bad quality, and one which is often overlooked by those trying to promote some message or key idea. Indeed, Matthews (1984) argues that

> So much emphasis has been placed on the development of children's abilities, especially their cognitive abilities, that we automatically assume their thinking is primitive and in need of being developed toward an adult norm. What we take to be primitive, however, may actually be more openly reflective than the adult norm we set.
>
> (Matthews, 1984, p. 52)

Thoughtful Children

Practitioners of philosophy with children such as Matthews and Lipman are not alone in their criticism of Piaget and stage maturation theories, in terms of children's rationality and reasoning abilities; Prout and James recognize this weakness in Piaget's theory and claim it is '... the mark of adult rationality. Within such a conceptual scheme children are marginalized beings awaiting temporal passage, through the acquisition of cognitive skill, into the social world of adults' (1997, p. 11). The problem remains, children are still not considered rational beings until they reach adulthood or adult status; Archard highlights that in the fullness of time children will be awarded this status – and it *is* a status since one is guaranteed a degree of autonomy and self-governance when one acquires it. He says that 'In the normal course of events children will *become* rational, autonomous adults' (1993, p. 53).

There is an arrogance in the assumption that children cannot and do not think as well as adults, or even that they aspire to attain adult thought – whatever that may be. Certainly, in expressing itself a child *may* have more of a limited vocabulary than an individual who has had more time to expand his/her vocabulary, yet this does not in any way allow that the thinking itself is diminished in some way; for the thinker the thought still exists whether expressed and shared audibly or not. MacMurray would hold that in a baby rationality is already in existence – 'His rationality is already present, though only germinally' (1970, p. 51). One may suppose a baby cannot be rational at birth as there is little for it to reason about having such minimal experience of the world and others around it. In fact, Piaget maintains that children should only be given answers which they '... are ready to assimilate and understand' (Pulaski, 1980, p. 101). We cannot, however, expect children to 'think further' when boundaries are placed in the way of their intellectual activities. It appears to be the adult who decides or dictates what children are ready to 'assimilate and understand' and there equally appears to be no such boundary or limit placed upon the reasoning or thinking of adult individuals. Matthews suggests that what often happens when talking with children is that adults do not '... discuss matters we ourselves find difficult or problematic' (1984, p. 1). Implicit within this behaviour is the idea that the child could not contribute positively to the thinking or reasoning and that he/she could not and would not understand the complexities underlying the topic. In essence, there appears to be something of a power relation where adults are in control and children are not given to see that the adult does not have all the answers. There is evidence of this displacement of power being the case with the invention of the printing press in the middle of the fifteenth century. Postman (1994) argues that with

the advent of the printing press and movable type a division
occurred between adults and children that had not previously been
there – one that shifted the balance of power.

It was adults who held the key to this new and literate world as

> Literature of all kinds – including maps, charts, contracts and deeds –
> collects and keeps valuable secrets. Thus in a literate world to be an
> adult implies having access to cultural secrets codified in unnatural
> symbols. In a literate world children must *become* adults by learning to
> read. But in a nonliterate world there is no need to distinguish sharply
> between the child and the adult, for there are few secrets.
>
> (Postman, 1994, p. 13)

Knowing Children

Postman extends his consideration of information providers in their
shaping of the adult/child divide to look at television. In our
modern age television is reversing the process set in place by print;
it is blurring the division between the adult and the child. He
raises three points which contribute to this blurring and they are
all concerned with accessibility: '... first, because it requires no
instruction to grasp its form; second, because it does not make
complex demands on either mind or behaviour; and third, because
it does not segregate its audience' (*ibid.*, p. 80). We are all provided
in this multi-media age with the same information, or at the very
least, have equal access to it. Secrets no longer exist in the way they
did when children could not access literature – of whichever genre
– the knowledge gap is closing. With the advent of the printing
press Postman would argue that

> Children are a group of people who do *not* know certain things that
> adults know. [However] In the Middle Ages there were no children
> because there existed no means for adults to know exclusive infor-
> mation. In the Age of Gutenberg, such a means developed. In the Age
> of Television, it is dissolved.
>
> (*ibid.*, p. 85)

One need not expand on how this division will become almost completely invisible as the internet takes a firmer hold on our societies. Postman has suggested that in the Middle Ages childhood ended at the age of seven as this is the time he considers children have command over speech. In essence, they can say and understand all that an adult can say and understand. Of course, there will be experiences a younger individual may not have direct knowledge of, but this is different to being able to reason as reason does not require experience, just an ability to reflect. Hendrick posits that while children have less developed minds than adults – in a biological sense – '... they have the same mechanisms for thought as adults do' (1997, p. 52) and will ultimately understand the world in the same way that adults do. Bearing in mind that within society our lives are guided by an accepted moral code, we must be processing or rationalizing our world in a similar way – which is not to say that we hold the same tenets about that society or world, merely that the function we use in order to consider it works in the same way for all of us, of whatever age.

In reflecting upon our moral codes in light of this reasoning capacity, it is not strictly accurate to suggest that one must be taught right and wrong, good and evil. It was suggested previously that we have a sense of right/wrong, good/evil, we have our own moral code and must – usually when young – be inducted into the *accepted* moral code of the larger majority; we undergo a process of socialization. It is this process that facilitates our smooth passage into the social realm where we are expected to interact with other human beings and behave in an appropriate manner. Elkin and Handel suggest that '... every society expends some of its resources to produce children who will become law-abiding adults' (1978, p. 33), adults who will live in an 'appropriate manner'. This living in an 'appropriate manner' is one where an individual has agreed to live by the majority moral code, however, we never so much agree as learn that this is how society functions and we must follow that path if we want to maintain our status and positive treatment within that society. We are not, however, following this path blindly, and children will not do this either. In accepting the rule that we agree to live by the accepted majority moral code, we do not renounce the ability or capacity or opportunity to question it. Reason, it might be said, comes into effect when one has to defend one's moral code, and this defence may be exhibited in 'bad' behaviour. 'Bad' behaviour can manifest itself in children as well as in adults, *it* does not recognize age barriers, but those others with whom we live and interact in society do. For instance, if a child sees fit to exhibit his or her disagreement with something by refusing to move from his/her seat he/she is perceived as being spoiled, cheeky, naughty or downright bad. If an adult decides to display his or her dissatisfaction in a similar manner then that individual, while perhaps causing a nuisance (the desired effect) will be perceived as availing him/herself of the right to dissent and protest. This is a silent example, however, but the effect is the same in other, more vocal instances. If an adult asks a pertinent or searching question in relation to a moral code or other assumption which governs our lives he or she is seen as intelligent, probing and admirable; if children ask similar questions they are seen at best as cute and interesting and at worst as pests, nuisances and 'smarty pants'. In fact, children *do* frequently challenge or question the external and agreed moral code; consider how often one has experienced a young child persisting with 'why?' questions. The response the child receives is very different to that of the adult. The reasoning that accompanies the questioning has to be learned – we have the faculty but we need to practise with it, we have to utilize our reason like a mental bench-press.

Reasoning is not the same as questioning, but it is the first step; we must first set up the issue we wish to examine or ponder. Reasoning, it could be said, comes from the practice of defending one's moral code or questioning the moral code of another. Reasoning appears to be the *activity* which takes place when one is confronted by an idea – be that a moral code or otherwise – that does not resonate with one's own and where the individuals concerned defend or, at the very least, project their stance – often with the aim of persuasion or clarification of the alternative point of view. There are those, of course, (and this may not necessarily imply children) who do not reason externally (or even internally) about their moral code – and it is only external reasoning in the form of argumentation that we can see or judge.

As Archard (1998) states in his discussion of Locke,

The adult does not differ significantly from the child in its basic cognitive abilities, it just has more time in which to reflect and more material upon which to reflect. The adult's reason is that of the child's come 'awake', and made 'visible'.

(Archard, 1998, p. 88)

Archard goes on to say that 'Children are born, in some sense, with or to reason, they develop through the normal course of nature into fully rational adults, and yet may be "moulded" into exercisers of reason' (*ibid.*, p. 91). This statement holds three problems. First, it implies that all adult human beings (whatever that may mean) are fully rational, that they have developed their reasoning capacity *and* practice in full. This is patently not the case, partly because there are obvious examples whereby an adult has demonstrated actions that are less than reasoned or rational and secondly, there is an assumption that we know – or can know – our full capacity and potential for reasoning and rationalizing. The third error that Archard makes is that he misuses the word 'moulded'. Not only are children 'moulded' into exercisers of reason in the sense that they are shown, taught and learn how to reason, but the important point that Archard fails to take account of is that the *results* of this reasoning itself, to put it simply, are 'moulded'. Younger, more pliable and malleable human beings have their reason, and thus their moral codes, moulded to suit that of the society into which they are expected to function. Archard – and indeed other philosophers – when talking of children and reason are discussing thinking in a specific way, they do not generally account for the possibility for abstract thought in the young individual and constrain reason to the realms of behavioural manifestations.

Jenks echoes this sentiment in his study of childhood as behavioural manifestations are how we measure those individuals within our society, and we subdivide that society into categories to facilitate this assessment process; Jenks says that 'The idea of childhood is not a natural but a social construct and as such its

status is constituted in particularly socially located forms of discourse' (1996, p. 29). As Cunningham (1995) states,

> The peculiarity of the late twentieth century, and the root cause of
> much present confusion and angst about childhood, is that a public
> discourse which argues that children are persons with rights to a
> degree of autonomy is at odds with the remnants of the romantic view
> that the right of the child is to be a child. The implication of the first
> is a fusing of the worlds of adult and child, and of the second the
> maintenance of separation.
>
> (Cunningham, 1995, p. 190)

It almost says nothing when one says 'the right of a child is to be a
child'. This statement presumably refers to young individuals in
our society being allowed to exist without the responsibilities one
has when one is older. And as Jenks says, in and of itself, a child is
nothing; however, in the context of the society within which we are
now placed, a meaning has been created, but not particularly
articulated or explained. He adds that while childhood is being
understood as a social construct '... it makes reference to a social
status delineated by boundaries incorporated within the social
structure and manifested through certain typical forms of conduct'
(1982a, p. 12). There is a certain conduct expected of children
when they are being children; it maintains their status as people
lacking power. Jenks maintains that

> ... children are locked, for their intelligibility, within the contingency
> of social conventions. The negotiable character of these conventions is
> a question of power, which children can only exercise in partial form.
> They can demand attention but not redefinition.
>
> (1996, p. 123)

Child's Play

One must wonder how an entity can demand redefinition if that
entity has a status in society such that it possesses a role composed
of expected behaviours. Prout and James highlight the social

conceptualization of childhood: 'The immaturity of children is a biological fact of life but the ways in which this immaturity is understood and made meaningful is a fact of culture' (1997, p. 7), and one of the ways this cultural shaping of children is promoted is through play.

Children are kept in the playground, it is the child's 'right to be a child' which generally, somewhere along the line, seems to mean he/she should be allowed to play. This, however, is another subversive socialization tactic. Denzin holds that ' "Play" is a fiction from the adult world' (1982, p. 192). In saying that the idea of play is created by adults what Denzin means is that when children are on their own they create their own social worlds and social orders, it is interpreted by 'outsiders' – adults – as play because they perhaps do not recognize – or do not want to recognize – the constructed social orders that have been invented, manipulated or simply maintained. In suggesting that play is subversive it can be so in two different ways; first, in the way we interpret what children are doing when left to their own devices and secondly, in the way their world and environment is constructed for them, in what they are given and how they are interacted with by adults when playing in order that they learn the *accepted* social order. At one time girls were given dolls to nurse and aprons to wear when playing 'house', while boys were given guns and construction kits – this is the way the adult world functioned; women stayed at home minding baby and keeping house while men went out to work or to protect in order to provide for the 'weaker sex'. Little has changed; certainly we have moved from this gender stereotyping somewhat, but we still give children the 'toys' we see as valuable and worthwhile in their preparation for fitting into the social order that has been created and maintained by those adults in society. Prout and James (1997) discuss the view taken by developmental psychologists of play and how they – the psychologists – see this play as more rational as the child becomes older and that the child interacts in a more intellectually 'mature' manner:

> The decreasing 'irrationality' of children's play as they mature is taken
> [by developmental psychologists] as a measure of evolving 'rationality'

of thought, charting the ways in which 'primitive' concepts become replaced by sophisticated ideas.

(Prout and James, 1997, p. 11)

It is interesting to note that the games adults play are never seen to diminish the rationality of the participants, at worst they are simply accused of being 'childish' or 'child-like', and this is a negative perception or ascription. One is encouraged to believe that through socialization and direction toward certain forms of behaviour one will become more rational, more acceptable in and to society and therefore more likely to become an adult. Adulthood is seen almost as some kind of reward for having kept the rules of childhood and for having learned the ones to permit entry to adulthood. Prout *et al.* compare this passive and conforming entity – child – to a laboratory rat, the child has survived the maze of socialization and has learned how to retrieve the treat at the end of the maze – in this case the treat is adulthood:

> Socialization is the process which magically transforms the one into the other, the key which turns the asocial child into a social adult. The child's nature is therefore assumed to be different; for the model to work indeed this must be the case.

(*ibid.*, p. 13)

Shamgar-Handelman (1994) is another who considers childhood to be a social construction, but also raises a very important point in the search for a definition of the concept of 'child':

> Childhood is a social phenomenon. It is so in the sense that every society crystallizes its own set of norms, rules and regulations which dictate its attitudes towards the category of its members defined as children. This attitude towards children stems from the highest moral values of society that define the essence of a person. The most prominent characteristic of a *child*, according to any definition, is that he/she is not (yet) an *adult*.

(Shamgar-Handelman, 1994, p. 250)

The important aspect of this definition is not that a child is not yet an adult as there appears to be no explicit definition of what an adult is, but the key word in her explanation or definition is *person*; she talks of society defining a person by high moral values and it would seem that Shamgar-Handelman perceives adult and person as one and the same thing. We should return to what was said previously in order to consider whether child meets this criterion for adulthood.

Conclusions

It has been shown in this chapter that developmental psychologists such as Piaget would disregard philosophical thinking or reasoning in young individuals as 'romancing' and that there does not appear to be a clear distinction between adult and child thinking. Contrary to the developmentalists' perspective, children are as perfectly capable of reasoning about their world as many adults. In fact, they frequently call into question moral codes that are different to their own, while at the same time being able to reason about the code they hold. This chapter has seen how social obedience and an 'acceptable' adult is produced as a result of the socialization of the child and his/her moral code in order that an individual moral code is tailored to suit that of the majority moral code, the one the current society lives by. The idea of child is a construction of society, one designed to establish power relations and one which does not necessarily treat children as persons, as ends in themselves.

5

Are Children Persons?

In this chapter we return to some of the concepts previously considered. In the first instance we look again at the notion of person in light of our chosen definition: an individual is a person if they treat others as such. This is considered more closely in relation to children and their place in a moral society especially in terms of motivation and one's perception of right and wrong. We also return to the discussion regarding personal identity and the idea of a continuous personal identity. The question of whether one is the same person as one was previously will be considered in conjunction with a consideration of how one's actions – since they are moral – may determine whether or not, or in what ways, one is the same person.

Consider Matthews, who suggests that 'Children are people, fully worthy of both the moral and intellectual respect due persons. They should be respected for what they are, as well as what they can become' (1994, p. 122); thus accepting the Ancients' idea of potentiality, but also bringing the respect due forward in time within the life of the individual. Here, though, Matthews appears to be suggesting that if children are due the same respect as persons then they themselves are also persons. Is this the case? Are young human beings persons? As McCall says, 'In many cultures the properties attributable to persons are not ascribed to children' (1990, p. 10). This is a crucial point in trying to define 'child'.

The notion of 'child' has been cultivated over these last two or three hundred years to influence behaviours – the behaviour of our older members of society and that of the younger members. In some ways it may also be used as a tool or excuse to explain away the behaviour of the younger humans, behaviour that is perhaps more 'animal', closer to nature – and we, as humans, like to think or believe we are far removed from the animalness of our nature, hence in our societies we form rules and notions of behaviour that we expect others to live by. I would agree with Jenks (1996) when he states that

> Childhood is to be understood as a social construct, it makes reference to a social status delineated by boundaries that vary through time and from society to society but which are incorporated within the social structure and thus manifested through and formative of certain typical forms of conduct. Childhood then always relates to a particular cultural setting.
>
> (Jenks, 1996, p. 7)

This then partly explains why the concept of 'child' has changed so considerably in the last few centuries, not even so much changed, as has been invented, and invented by persons!

The Way to Personhood

Let us consider how the term person was defined previously. A person, it was stated, is a given title, a role which one is given at birth. A person is one who belongs to or resides in a society – and in living within that society or community the individual is accepting that he/she should live by the relevant moral codes – although the acceptance is implicit as one has been socialized into it. A person, further, has a conscience, a faculty for determining right from wrong and good from bad and the individual uses this conscience in line with his or her reasoning ability to link with the moral codes established by the society. It is clear that at birth one is born into a society or community; it may not be so evident that the moral codes held in that society are ones held by the young individual but they will quickly learn the ones that have been deemed acceptable. Previously it was suggested that conscience was 'in-built'; we are conceived and come into the external world with a faculty for determining our set of moral codes that go toward making us who we are and what we will become. The fact that as a young child one may not articulate these codes (for a variety of reasons) is immaterial; it could even be said that the only time moral codes are articulated aloud is when they conflict with another code one has encountered. As Matthews (1994) states,

> ...long before a child will have to deal with moral dilemmas, let alone give a justification for reasoning a dilemma, the child can have a strong emphatic response to the victims of suffering, or injustice, and a working understanding of central paradigms for terms of moral assessment.
>
> (Matthews, 1994, p. 65)

These examples, however, are more than empathy, they are firmly grounded in the moral codes of the child, and they know something to be right or wrong, good or bad in a sense that they do not have the capacity to, as yet, articulate. This lack of articulacy comes, not from any absence of moral feeling or thinking, but from an absence of the necessary oral language. As Taylor (1989) posits,

> A pattern can exist just in the dos and don'ts that people accept and mutually enforce without there being (yet) an explicit rationale. And as children, we learn some of the most fundamental patterns at first just as such. The articulations come later.
>
> (Taylor, 1989, p. 204)

Finally, a person is one who behaves towards others as though they too were persons. Altogether, this suggests that this is the way in which society 'works', that one has to learn one's role in order to become an adult, that person equals adult; childhood is a period of training and learning. As Shamgar-Handelman (1994) holds,

> ...childhood should be described as that period of time in each person's life which society allocates for the process of training to become the kind of member that the society wants him/her to be....

During this period, different agencies of society are expected to ensure that the child will be transformed into an adult in accordance with the adult-image acceptable in that society.

(Shamgar-Handelman, 1994, p. 250)

And what is the end – and desired – result? Adulthood. *Full* personhood!

Purdy reflects that

Children probably acquire empathic emotions through simple classical conditioning. They learn adaptive social behaviours partly by experiencing the consequences of their own actions and partly by observing the sequences of interaction engaged in by other people.

(Purdy, 1998, p. 196)

She goes on to add that

This view conceives of children as unfinished beings who need a period of development and teaching to become mature human beings. It requires a clear conception of traits we find admirable; it concedes that they are unlikely to develop if not explicitly taught.

(*ibid.*, p. 197)

This, it would seem, is the level at which society primarily functions in relation to children. Jenks states the problem clearly, 'The child's serious purpose and our intentions towards him or her are dedicated to a resolution of that initial paradox by transforming him or her into an adult like ourselves' (1996, p. 3) – yet another example of how children are not seen as persons; although in Chapter 1 it was held that to be a person one had to treat others as such. Now if we, as adults, behave towards our younger neighbours in a way that will result in producing an 'acceptable' adult, then in some sense we are treating the child as a person as we are behaving towards them as though they would behave towards us in a similar manner. However, one might suggest that the child in this instance is not being treated as a person if we are to follow Kant, as we are here behaving toward the child as a means to an end, which would ultimately compromise *our* personhood.

As persons we are bound by society, we have an obligation to care for our children, to feed them, clothe them and nurture them. If we consider that as persons we are 'code keepers' of a moral code that proclaims we must not kill, and we must value each other individually, then it is our duty to protect and provide for those not yet able to protect and provide for themselves, those – to a certain extent – who are dependent on others for their *physical* well-being. As Archard suggests, 'Children could not surely have a lesser moral status than animals' (1998, p. 96), and we go to great lengths to provide for our domestic pets, protect our wild animals and their habitats and maintain a certain level of accommodation and treatment towards our farm animals. Kant, in the words of Zweig, held that this responsibility for those dependent on us was one we are morally bound to, even in the smallest community – that of the family – 'The union of two persons, husband and wife, leads to the duty to care for and sustain their children as persons; children have an innate right to be cared for by their parents' (1998, p. 127).

Kant suggests that it is a right that one has to be cared for, rather – I would posit – it is a duty one has to care. Jenks would also disagree with Kant – to a certain extent – with his idea that caring for a dependent child is necessarily natural in its thrust, he is '... not arguing that altruism or care that the adult feels towards the child is itself a unitary or a "natural" feeling – no, rather I would suggest that it is a social construction' (1996, p. 41). This, it could be held, is something that has developed since the emergence of childhood as a concept in the seventeenth century, a time when childcare changed from wet-nursing and fostering out one's young until they were less dependent (in certain social circles) to one – perhaps as a result of Locke and Rousseau's writings – where the child was recognized as a valued individual with its own status in society. In the new politics that emerged with this new awareness of the child, adults approached children and child-rearing differently. 'In an efficient, "caring" society child-rearing and education liberate the individual into compliance' (*ibid.*, p. 43) says Jenks.

Compliant Children

This social compliance is learned from, and through, others and experience – as Rousseau suggested. The parents are the first key influences on the child's behaviour; the first 'test' of the child's moral code. In fact, as Phillips suggests in his introduction to Ariès' *Centuries of Childhood*, 'Once you invent the child you need something – like a school or a family – to contain it' (1996, p. 8). The family and school are the generally accepted institutions for modelling behaviour and initiating children into the adult/person world. Cunningham reinforces this notion; 'It is undoubtedly chiefly within the family that children learned about the world into which they had been born, and about the roles they could expect to play' (1995, p. 99). Although Cunningham was referring to past centuries, his thesis still holds today. In fact, while children learn – from family and school – what roles they will be expected to play, Cunningham fails to acknowledge that being a child is actually a role also. There are rules involved, and expected patterns of behaviour that a child would be expected to exhibit or perform. Jenks picks up on this very point: 'The status of childhood has its boundaries maintained through the crystallization of conventions and discourses into lasting institutional forms like families, nurseries, schools and clinics, all agencies specifically designed and established to process the child as a uniform entity' (1996, p. 5).

Shields asks the question 'How can a child acquire a custom of normative behaviour when it does not yet possess the requisite norms of correct and incorrect behaviour?' (1998, p. 170). The answer, quite simply, is that the 'correct' and 'incorrect' behaviours are learned as the child is born into a social environment and structure where there are those who have already learned and/or accepted these behaviour structures.

Purdy suggests that 'Rousseau generally emphasized children's internal "program", arguing that it flowers but with minimal interference by us, whereas Locke's *tabula rasa* underscored the critical importance of environmental pressures' (1998, p. 194). Rousseau, in *Emile*, makes plain that the child is initiated into the external world through habit and taps the world he or she already understands:

> The child's first mental experiences are purely affective, he is only aware of pleasure and pain; it takes him a long time to acquire the definite sensations which show him things outside himself, but before these things present and withdraw themselves, so to speak, from his sight, taking size and shape for him, the recurrence of emotional experiences is beginning to subject the child to the rule of habit.
>
> (Rousseau, 1948, p.29)

Rousseau embarked upon his theoretical project with *Emile*, becoming Emile's preceptor when the boy was at a young age and aiding his development or evolution into a grown man. Rousseau held that

> Nature would have them children before they are men. If we try to invert this order we shall produce a forced fruit immature and fla-vourless, fruit which will be rotten before it is ripe; we shall have young doctors and old children. Childhood has its own ways of seeing, thinking and feeling; nothing is more foolish than to try and sub-stitute our ways.
>
> (*ibid.*, p. 54)

Rousseau evidently had a clear idea of what he was trying to achieve, trying to produce.

Initially Rousseau would hold that

> We are born capable of learning, but knowing nothing, perceiving nothing. The mind, bound up with imperfect and half grown organs, is not even aware of its own existence. The movements and cries of the new-born child are purely reflex, without knowledge and will.
>
> (*ibid.*, p. 28)

This directly contradicts what Rousseau also states – that the child is aware of pleasure and pain. Certainly the avoidance of pain may be a reflex or reaction, but to seek pleasure surely implies some sense of intentionality. In his 'experiment' Rousseau believed

'Man's proper study is that of his relation to his environment. So long as he only knows that environment through his physical nature, he should study himself in relation to things; this is the business of childhood' (*ibid.*, p. 175). He goes on to say that 'The further we are from the state of nature, the more we lose our natural tastes; or rather, habit becomes a second nature, and so completely replaces our real nature, that we have lost all knowledge of it' (*ibid.*, p. 115).

One must, however, question just how natural Emile's education is. The preceptor appears to manipulate and contrive the 'natural' conditions for Emile's learning; as Simon suggests, 'If the preceptor plants objects for Emile's "natural" curiosity to explore, then the curiosity itself is cultivated and formed by the one who controls the objects' (1998, p. 118). It could be argued that this is still, to a certain extent, the case in our educational system today, that there is an expected and desired outcome and the preceptor/teacher and parents are in cahoots to attain it.

Moral Children

Simon holds that '... the insistence on an education from things, designed to protect Emile's negative freedom, leaves him with a conception of self ill-suited for life in a community' (*ibid.*, p. 117). One may wish to see as a flaw in Rousseau's model of education the absence of any kind of moral 'conditioning', any influence of Emile's moral code, in order that he may function effectively and acceptably as part of a larger society. Certainly this would be a flaw in terms of what is expected of our current educational system. Simon suggests that

> Given the emphasis on Emile's independence and the attempt to reproduce the state of nature during his early childhood, it comes as no surprise that the only 'moral' lesson that actually occurs during this period involves the concept of property. This lesson avoids the traps of teaching abstract concepts of right and wrong, or interfering in

Emile's 'natural' development by imposing outside ideas not derived from experience.

(ibid., p. 111)

She also suggests that if Rousseau intended to teach the concepts of right and wrong, good and bad, he'd have had to impose rules, sanctions and restrictions on certain of Emile's actions; she believes this to be negative in the sense that 'Without an awareness that his actions produce certain moral consequences, Emile's moral education remains stalled' (*ibid.*, p. 109). I would go further, and would suggest to Rousseau, that Emile should be made aware that *all* his actions are moral in the sense that the outcome or consequences of such actions have some bearing on society and those that constitute it. And, as Simon says, 'Emile cannot internalize the moral law if it is never explicitly externalized' (*ibid.*, p. 111). Rousseau, it could be argued, would suggest that Emile, and by implication other children too, lack any sense of morality as they lack reason. In *Emile* Rousseau states that 'Reason alone teaches us to know good and evil. Therefore, conscience, which makes us love the one and hate the other, though it is independent of reason, cannot develop without it.' He continues, 'Before the age of reason we do good or ill without knowing it, and there is still no morality in our actions, although there is something in our feelings with regard to other people's actions in relation to ourselves' (1948, p. 34).

He compounds this by saying that '. . . until the age when the reason becomes enlightened, when growing emotion gives a voice to conscience, what is wrong for young people is what those have decided to be wrong' (*ibid.*, p. 344). This is no different than for any other individual, no matter their age. It is simply the case that we are trained out of our codes that deviate from the accepted ones and our 'childish' reason is given little credence if we are to question and disagree with the accepted mode of being.

McCall discusses Dennett and says that

In outlining the conditions an entity must satisfy to be judged a person, Dennett makes use of the notion of an Intentional System. An Intentional System is a system whose behaviour can be explained by ascribing to it intentional predicates such as those concerned with beliefs, desires, hopes and fears.

(McCall, 1990, p. 71)

The young individuals in our society certainly appear to exhibit these traits: a belief in Santa Claus or God; a desire to be with other human beings; a hope for certain birthday presents or a visit from a favourite relative or friend; a fear of the dark, of a parent going away not to return later. These are perhaps simple examples, but when one tries to think of 'adult' beliefs, desires, hopes or fears they are no less trivial sounding – or different even – when articulated. However, as McCall notes, Dennett has

> ...omitted children from the status of personhood, despite the fact that the conditions he has outlined are empirical conditions, and hence any judgments about whether a being fulfils the conditions needs to be made on evidence. Dennett does not provide such evidence.
>
> (*ibid.*, p. 90)

McCall maintains that Dennett would hold that '... to be a moral agent is to be an agent who is capable of actions which are both "right" and "wrong", under whatever ethical system the agent recognises' (*ibid.*, p. 86). As previously stated, we all have a notion of right and wrong and therefore must recognize what we believe to be right or wrong. Further, as humans, we are certainly all *capable* of 'actions which are both "right" and "wrong"' – the fact that one does not always act upon one's capabilities does not mean that the innateness and potential for the action is not there. In fact, the rightness or wrongness of an action can only be judged against what is deemed by society to be right or wrong. Mayo (1986) suggests that

> A good action is not the same as a right action. There are complex relations and dependencies between the good and the right (and their opposites). A wrong action may be one that produces harm. A good man is one who tends to do right actions because they are right. A

good action is done with a good motive, or such as a good man would do.

(Mayo, 1986, p. 40)

And it is this motivation or intention to which we must now turn.

If we are to believe that children are non-rational or pre-rational beings then we can only say that all actions are *intended* to be right or good actions because the child will only voluntarily do what it thinks is right, for if it cannot reason then it cannot reflect upon the rightness or wrongness of an action and its consequences. For if we recall Mayo, he claims that 'One can't admit something is wrong while saying in the same breath that one doesn't care whether it is or not' (*ibid.*, p. 13). If, on the other hand, we are willing to grant children the ability to reason and/or be rational individuals, then we must equally allow that they may have a range of motivations, as adults do; it may be that they will clean their room for extra pocket money, they may work hard at school for a trip to the swimming pool, they will tell the truth in order not to be punished, they may be 'nice' to their brothers and sisters in order that the brothers and sisters are 'nice' to them in return. Adult motivation for doing 'right' actions is no different; they may work hard in order to receive payment, they may pay their bills in order not to be punished and they may be 'nice' to other individuals in order that the others are 'nice' in return. Earlier it was suggested that intentions can only ever be thought of as good intentions, one could not desire something to be bad – perhaps for another individual, but not for oneself, in which case the intention is still good, selfish perhaps, but good nonetheless – and that it was motivations that may be good or bad. We – and this is the same for all individuals of whatever category – may all be motivated by different things, but the most interesting example that was suggested was that one will treat others well in order that one may receive similar treatment – and this is precisely what was meant earlier with reference to treating others as persons being what makes one a person. So, whatever the motivation – be it a reward of a packet of sweets, familial love, the desire to do well in the workplace – one *is* a person if one treats others as such and children *do* behave towards others as persons. If this, then, is our definition of person – that one treats others as persons, that one abides by a moral code and one can reason about one's moral code and that of others – then a child is indeed a person. However, one may wonder if one is the *same* person throughout one's whole life.

Continuous Children

If we consider that we have perpetrated various right actions and wrong actions throughout the course of our lives, and our personhood depends on the way we treat others, one may 'lose' one's personhood for a time, at the instant of the wrong act, but this does not necessarily mean that one is no longer a person for the rest of one's life; it seems to be the case that one cannot be a person, or the *same* person, over a length of time. One can never be described as a *bad* person, however, because implicit within the definition of person one can only perpetrate good or right actions. So is Warnock correct when she says that in asking 'Am I the same person as I was forty years ago?' one is answering the question with the question 'For if "I" is intelligibly used twice in this question, then obviously the reference *must* be the same' (Warnock, 1992, p. 202)? Similarly, we saw in a previous chapter that we believe we are the same individual because others tell us so in the ways they recognize us and relate to us. For Spinoza the nature of an infant and a grown man were different, but despite this difference in nature '... he has observed that other men remain the same men from infancy to adulthood' (Morrison, 1994, p. 35) and in observing this about others one can assume the same about oneself. There are several thought experiments that one could apply to the question of continuous personal identity in relation to the problem of children and adults. If we consider Gillett's discussion of Parfit's tele-transporter 'experiment'

I am in some way replaced by, or made to give rise to, a fully-fledged psychological replica of myself, complete with memory and character. I am asked whether this would be me, or even more suggestively, whether I could consider myself to be myself after such replication. I am then asked to consider what would happen if two such replicas were produced. It is argued that, if identity is what is important in the first case, then the production of a second replica would completely confound what is important, because I could not be identical to two individuals who would subsequently lead separate lives.

(Gillett, 1987, p. 79)

The experiment is false. As Warnock showed that in using 'I' twice in her question about being the same person after 40 years, Parfit's experiment falls foul on the same grounds. If I were to be asked if the replica is me then one has to wonder what – or who – it is that is being questioned. So, if *I* am being questioned and I am *me* then there is no sense in which I could answer that the replica is *me* because if it was the replica would equally be able to answer – and it can't. Even if the replica did answer thinking it was me, and to everyone else it may well be, *I* would know that it was not since I am more than my memory and character which are the bits that remained intact in the experiment.

One may indeed be a different person over time, but this is often a linguistic confusion. I may be a different person in terms of the actions I have undertaken or the codes to which I have adhered – or not – but the question is whether or not my *identity* remains the same and this is more than my personhood. Even in talking of *my* personhood one can see that there is something to which person-hood belongs. Rorty (1976b) suggests

...it might be helpful to list some candidates for the 'I', indicating something of the range of contrasts – none of which entirely maps on to each other – in which it has served. It has been identified with the interior or internal perspective in contrast with the external; with the subjective in contrast with the objective; with the subject-of-experi-ence in contrast with its experiences; with rationality and will in contrast with causality and desire; with spontaneity and creativity in contrast with the conditioned; with the decider and agent in contrast with the predictor and observer; with the knower and the interpreter in contrast with the known and interpreted; with reflective consciousness in contrast with the content reflected; with mind in contrast with body.

(Rorty, 1976b, p. 12)

This notion of self that Locke (1976) earlier suggested can 'consider itself as itself' is what we are and, as Postman suggests 'In saying what we wish a child to become, we are saying what we are' (1994, p. 63) and it does not seem that we – adults – are any different. Jenks suggests that '. . . to abandon a shared category of the child is to confront a daunting paradox'; he sees childhood as serving to articulate '. . . not just the experience and status of the young within modern society but also the projections, aspirations, long-ings and altruism contained within the adult experience' (1996, p. 136). And if as adults we do just that, abandon our notion of child and childhood, Jenks goes on to ask '. . . what happens to the concept of "childhood" through which we, as adults, see ourselves and our society's past and future?' (*ibid.*, p. 136). Jenks need not worry about losing his notion of childhood – which implies a loss of 'child' since childhood is simply that time when one is a 'child'. In being able to project a future for oneself or any other individual – or a past or present – one is recognizing that one is a continuous individual in some sense.

Perhaps as a younger individual my identity is not so developed; after all I have not had a chance to practise or exercise it; Gillett (1987) talks about an identity becoming defined. He maintains

As a person's identity becomes defined, so the kind of story he tells about himself takes on a richness and a depth which draws on his cumulative experience of life. That he *can* tell such a story suggests that his life and identity is more like a painting or a novel than a heap of sand or a string of contingently connecting events. The resulting composition is not merely a 'stream of consciousness' liable to all the twists and vagaries found in dreams or reveries, but is profoundly influenced and formed by the empirical nature of persons and by their relations to an objective world.

(Gillett, 1987, p. 86)

The idea of one's identity being like a novel should not be confused with the notion that one cannot have a complete self until the end of one's life, until one has completed every experience one is liable to encounter. A child does have this self, and, like its reasoning, the identity of the child needs to be exercised. Indeed, in this fact children, again, are no different from their older counterparts. Jenks (1982a) reinforces this fact when he talks about the different growth metaphors that are used about children:

> The kind of 'growth' metaphors that are used in discussion about children are all of the character of what is yet to be ... thus childhood is spoken of as 'becoming', as a *tabula rasa*, as laying the foundations, taking on, growing up, preparation, inadequacy, inexperience, immaturity, and so on. Such metaphors all seem to speak of a relation to an unexplicated but nevertheless firmly established, rational adult world. This world is not only assumed to be complete and static, but also desirable.
>
> (Jenks, 1982a, p. 13)

Rousseau makes an important and very relevant point when he talks about becoming a part of that desirable society, that 'You will find he [Emile] has a few moral ideas concerning his present state and none concerning manhood; what use could he make of them, for the child is not, as yet, an active member of society' (1948, p. 125).

What does this mean, to be an active member of society? Rousseau was not the only writer at the time making this point; as Archard claims, 'Locke writes of children as the recipients of an ideal upbringing, citizens in the making, fledgling but imperfect reasoners, and blank sheets filled by experience' (1998, p. 85). Locke went on to consider that parents had power over their children because children did not possess the rights of adult citizens. Cunningham goes further back in time to what may have influenced Locke's perspective on child: 'The overriding impression derived from ancient sources is that childhood was not seen as important for itself, but as part of a process towards producing a good citizen' (1995, p. 25). So, even in the times when children mingled freely with the adults, there was another notion that acted as a divider, that of citizen, an actively participating member of society.

If we remember Lewis' example of Methuselah and his series of composite selves, we can compare our existence with his. Certainly I will not survive until I am 969 years old, but even if I reach 70 *I* will have had many experiences, thoughts and interactions; *I* will have that same recognizable aspect of my being that I have now or had when I was ten and it should be recognizable to others as well as to me. I may have had many personhoods as I will have reacted differently in a range of situations, but my identity, the part that is *me* will remain constant. In fact, should I commit a 'crime' tomorrow by breaking a moral code and am not found out for another ten years, should I be punished? Am I the same person? No, I am not the same person, because the person is the moral actor in me, but I am the same individual and should be treated as such. There may be instances when someone would not be convicted of a 'crime' as he/she did not have all of his/her mental faculties at the time of the incident because of some mental illness. This is a different argument because in that case the individual may have had no concept of the accepted moral code. Some may argue that children have no concept of the moral code, children who commit the 'worst' form of breaking a moral code – children who murder – and this suits the way children are categorized.

Perhaps not a pleasant thought, but there have always been children who murder, and doubtless there always will be, but society finds this particularly shocking. However, the members of society may find it less shocking if they acknowledged that there is basically very little difference between an adult and a child – murderer or not. Very often such children in this category are viewed differently; they are seen as something other than child. Jenks (1996) explains:

> ...by refusing children who commit acts of violence acceptance within the category of child, the public was reaffirming to itself [in light of the James Bulger case] the essence of what children are (and thereby also reaffirming its commitment to a 'shared' social order). That is, it was a way to restore the primary image of the innate

innocence of children through relegating some would-be children (those who commit acts of violence) to another category essentialized through images of evil or pathology. Thus, the stigma of anomaly works to explain how certain children are capable of actions which other, 'normal', children are not: the system of classification stays intact by resisting the 'defilement' of the abhorrent case.

(Jenks, 1996, p. 129)

By maintaining the category – or role – 'child', society is perpetrating the image of child as something less than adult. Jenks suggests that we make the child less strange by transforming him/her into an adult. This notion of child in the state – or stage – of becoming is a negative one, one which reinforces the power structures, and one to which we will return in the following chapters.

Conclusions

It has been argued in this chapter that the notion of child is linked very closely with social status and the place children find themselves in within society. Certainly children find themselves in a place or social position, as they have extremely limited power, if they have any at all, to place themselves anywhere else. It appears that the purpose children serve is to learn to be adults, and adults of the 'correct' type with the appropriate and acceptable behaviour desired by the adults in control of society. It has been seen, however, that there are implications for the personhood of the carers of children, be they parents, teachers, policy makers, and the like; if one wants to maintain one's personhood then it is vital that he/she treats others as persons – this is not always the case with respect to how children are treated. It was important in this chapter to give consideration to the idea that children themselves exist in a space of moral issues and that their intentions and motivations play as much a part in the shaping of their identities as they do for adults. In fact, it is merely the lack of social status that disqualifies children from being perceived as moral agents – or at the very least, as moral agents with acceptable moral codes. From the outset children are socialized first by their families and then by the school – an agency of the State – in order that they acquire the desired behaviours. We have seen that in the language of socialization and in talking of children generally, growth metaphors and language which imply – or even explicitly state – development or becoming are used. This reinforces the notion that children are in some way less than adults; their status is consolidated as one below that of fully-fledged adulthood, that state to which they should aspire. Further, while discussing this idea of growth or development the concept of the citizen was briefly introduced; this will be taken up again in Chapter 6.

While children are expected to desire this adult status, or rather, that this is what they are being groomed for, some time was given to the question of continuous personal identity. Using Parfit's teletransporter 'experiment' and Lewis' example of Methuselah, it was shown that one's personhood may change over time, but that one's identity remains constant. If I talk of 'me' or 'I' then I can only be talking about the same thing every time, for if I was someone or something else I would not be me. So while we may talk about growing up or being a different person as an adult to what one was as a child, we may not be wrong. However, one would still be the same individual with the same identity – this is continuous.

6

The Citizen in Community

In this chapter the notion of citizenship is given further consideration. The participative nature of being a citizen will be shown to be linked strongly with the idea of community and working for a common goal or purpose. It will be made clear that in being a citizen one has a set of duties or responsibilities which one should adopt in order to be afforded the rights or privileges awarded by a society or community. The idea of citizens' juries and the importance of being a critical and reflective thinker in one's citizen role will also be introduced here.

Jenks, in the previous chapter, was seen to suggest that the category or role of child is in some way divisive and exclusive to certain members of society; the notion – and the behaviour displayed toward those who inhabit the notion – of child creates some form of distance between those perceived of as being adults and those seen as children. The child is not (yet) an adult, a full member of society – and this is the point of issue. While we can suggest that the child has personhood, it is disenfranchized within the society in which it lives. According to the United Nations Convention on the Rights of the Child one becomes an adult at age 18. This presents us with some confusion. In Scotland an individual may marry at age 16, but cannot make some decisions or vote on issues concerning his/her married life for a further two years. So, while it is possible to be a *person* before one is 18, it seems unlikely that one is able to play a full role in society; and in saying that one is not (yet) an adult what is really meant is that one is not (yet) a citizen. Faulks (2000) maintains that

Unlike slaves, vassals or subjects, whose statuses imply hierarchy and domination, citizens formally enjoy legitimate and equal membership of a society. If it is to have substance, therefore, citizenship cannot allow arbitrary treatment: citizens must be judged by objective and transparent criteria.

(Faulks, 2000, p. 4)

Certainly, one would not consider slaves, vassals or subjects to be synonymous, but can we be sure that they are not citizens? Can we be sure that *all* citizens are regarded as equal members of a society? We cannot be sure, I would argue, until we are able to say what a citizen *is*.

The Citizen Role

Being a citizen is necessarily bound up with belonging to a society. Through Socrates, Plato suggests that 'Society originates, then ... so far as I can see, because the individual is not self-sufficient, but has many needs which he can't supply himself' (1987a, p. 58). As human animals we need to belong to a group, and it is this *belongingness* that is important. In a sense we do not simply belong by being *part* of a group, we are, to some extent, *owned* by the society or group. This notion of ownership implies some function, some responsibility is necessary. For instance, if I own a car, I expect it to start in the morning, to get me from A to B and to have a boot large enough to carry my shopping from the supermarket. Certainly this way of considering the problem may be difficult in that one cannot suggest a car has the cognitive capacity to understand its purpose, never mind the moral agency to accept responsibilities. A better way to illustrate this may be to think in terms that I belong to a family and as such there are certain things expected of and from me: I should love my parents, help with celebratory dinners, send birthday cards and undertake some babysitting. Of course, different families will have different responsibilities or expectations, but there is some relation between the constituent members that makes the small family society similar to the larger society within which we function. Rousseau too follows the line that it is human need that creates the necessity – which is more than a desire – for society: 'The mind, as well as the body, has its needs: those of the body are the basis for society, those of the mind its ornaments' (1973, p. 4). As animals we need food and shelter and rarely is it the case that one might provide all these things without the need for others. Even in isolation one will have some dependency on the 'outside world' in terms of finding the tools with which to make one's shelter. Humans need society to furnish themselves with the goods for practical living, and a society of collective individuals is what is called for. However, to what is it we belong? Faulks posits that 'The status of citizen implies a sense of inclusion into the wider community. It recognises the contribution a particular individual makes to that community, while at the same time granting him or her individual autonomy' (2000, p. 4). So, not only is the physical inclusion a contributing factor in belonging to a society as a citizen, Faulks goes on to state that '. . . a key defining characteristic of citizenship, and what differentiates it from mere subjecthood, is an ethic of participation. Citizenship is an active rather than passive status ... Citizenship is always a reciprocal and, therefore, social idea' (*ibid.*, p. 4).

Reciprocity is the key. As a citizen one is expected – indeed bound – to participate in some form, but then, slaves participate in society, as do subjects. Within society everyone has their role to play; slaves, for instance, are responsible for undertaking hard labour or growing crops or tending to jobs that the owning classes do not wish to undertake themselves. However, rarely would a slave or servant be referred to as a citizen; there is something in citizenship which precludes the slave from having this role or name.

'The processes that determine how citizenship is defined are bound up with questions of self-interest, power and conflict' (*ibid.*, p. 7), says Faulks. Ancient Athens appears to have been the seat of democracy, and therefore citizenship. Through discussion and voting, citizens were part of the policy-making decisions in ancient Athens: 'Every citizen had an equal opportunity to state a case and influence decisions' (McCall, 1991, p. 36). It should be borne in mind, however, that in this context slaves and women were excluded from participating in what was an hereditary privilege. As Faulks (2000) indicates, it may still be the case that there is an imbalance in the citizenship status:

> It may be that women, for instance, are formally viewed as equal citizens with men. If, however, women exercise their citizenship within the constraints of a patriarchal system, in substantive terms their citizenship is worth less than that of men.
>
> (Faulks, 2000, p. 9)

It is not that women, in this instance, wish to participate less, but they are deterred from having as full a participation as men in the same environment and culture. One might say there is an enforced passivity for women with regards their citizenship status. Indeed, Faulks goes on to discuss the notion of passive citizens in eighteenth-century France as being '... those workers who could not afford to pay a citizens' tax of at least three days' pay and they were denied the opportunity to participate in the decision-making process' (*ibid.*, p. 34). He continues, 'If citizenship is to be truly inclusive we must acknowledge the need for a politics of difference' (*ibid.*, p. 86). This resonates somewhat with Rousseau's (1973) claim that

> ... there are two kinds of inequality among the human species; one which I call natural or physical, because it is established by nature, and consists in a difference of age, health, bodily strength, and the qualities of the mind or of the soul; and another, which may be called moral or political inequality, because it depends on a kind of convention, and is established, or at least authorized, by the consent of men. This latter consists of the different privileges which some men enjoy to the prejudice of others; such as that of being more rich, more honoured, more powerful, or even in a position to exact obedience.
>
> (Rousseau, 1973, p. 49)

It takes time for this system to establish itself from the foundations of a social group coming together to satisfy its needs. Rousseau's description of the foundations of society seems apt:

Men, who have up to now been roving in the woods, by taking a more settled manner of life, come gradually together, form separate bodies, and at length in every country arises a distinct nation, united in character and manner, not in regulations or laws, but by uniformity of life and food, and the common influence of climate. Permanent neighbourhood could not fail to produce, in time, some connection between different families.

(*ibid.*, p. 89)

Social Citizens

Certainly these social groupings will happen; even though individuals within such groupings may have different moral codes, the laws and regulations of the society will evolve from the codes that are held by the newly forming society. MacMurray (1970) highlights the notion that even within a society there are smaller groups with different moral codes:

> ...a large community may contain smaller communities within it, and the code of morality which is normal for the small community may be in a different mode from that which is normal for the larger. In other words, a man's apperception of his relations to the other members of his family may differ modally from his apperception of his relations as a citizen to other members of his State.
>
> (MacMurray, 1970, p. 122)

It is recognized that the needs of the individuals as humans are more important than the needs of individuals as citizens, and thus moral codes can influence the provision for those within the particular social context. Indeed, Denzin (1982) claims that societies are organized and ordered *by* the moral codes, this is what forms the structures of a society:

> Societies and people organize themselves into interacting moral orders: families and schools, rich people and poor people, the educated and the uneducated, the child and the adult. Relationships between

them are grounded in assumptions which justify the various social evaluations.

(Denzin, 1982, p. 189)

There are some societies, claims Faulks (2000), however, who do not need a concept of nationhood, such as the American Plains Indians, to feel a sense of obligation to one another. However, it could be argued that in this example it is merely that the Plains Indians see society or treat society as larger than the notion of society as villages, towns, cities or countries. It is in this sense of duty to one's fellow humans and in *acting* upon the sense that creates citizens. One must be active in relation to those within the community to be a citizen. However, it is in the nature of participation that may determine one's membership into society as a *citizen* – Mill states, 'He who does anything because it is the custom makes no choice' (1985, p. 122) and similarly, slaves can be very active members of a society, yet they are still not perceived as citizens. Slaves are not considered citizens perhaps because they act, not from a sense of duty or obligation, but another motivating factor; rather they are acting because they are compelled to perform in a certain way and undertake specific tasks. In other words, they have no choice.

Political Citizens

Faulks discusses the ancient *polis*, highlighting the issue that individuals recognized the close link '... between their own destinies and that of their community, rendering the notion of asserting one's rights against the interests of the wider community inconceivable' (2000, p. 17). The *polis* was prior to, and constitutive of the individual. Indeed, Aristotle suggests just this, 'For even the good of the community coincides with that of the individual, but the good of the community is clearly a greater and more perfect good both to get and to keep' (1955, p. 27). No one stands alone. There is a dependency built into the notion of society and as such we are, as persons, obliged to undertake some form of responsibility to the other members of our group. It is difficult to conceive of a society where there is little or no obligation between its members; as Faulks suggests, 'Citizenship is ... an excellent basis for human governance' (2000, p. 5), governance being the need to establish and maintain some form of social order. This social order may take a variety of forms, for instance, legislature, distribution of resources, protection, and so on. It is important in this participatory notion of citizenship to note that the interests of the citizen and the community itself are indivisible – this relates, again, to the idea of belonging. So important was the participation in decision-making that payments were made in ancient Athens to allow the poorer members of the community to take part. The Romans, on the other hand, claims Faulks, found that it was best to use citizenship as a '... tool of social control and pacification' (*ibid.*, p. 19). In some ways the current interest in citizenship is more akin to the Romans as more and more we find it being 'pushed' within education and the media as a 'cure-all' to society's ills. However, here, the notion of citizenship that is favoured is one where individuals are encouraged to be active citizens in their own right without the aspect of control and manipulation favoured by some. It is precisely in being an active member of a society or community which leads to effective citizenry. And here we take society as being a collection of people living together under the same rules and regulations; a community as being a collection of people working together towards a common 'good' while being bound to its society's rules and regulations. In talking of members of a society or community being 'active', it is assumed that one is not merely going about one's daily business of eating and sleeping; there are certain contributions one would be making were one to be considered active in a social setting. Contributions may take the form of working to bolster the economy, likewise spending money will aid the economic growth of the society, helping others by giving time or money develops the society and perhaps, and most importantly, in order to be an *active citizen* one must participate more vocally. One should be interacting with others to question, challenge and give voice to alternative moral codes, justifications or reasoning. One cannot be a passive citizen. Even in deliberately abstaining from voting one is acting in a mental and even physical sense by staying away from the polling station, but there is more to participation than voting. One may join focus groups, write letters to Members of Parliament, newspapers or other influential individuals or institutions. Even in discussing issues and topics relevant to the way one leads one's life one is being an active citizen, and in turn political. Indeed, Giroux may be cited in support of the notion that even in thinking and discussing and debating certain relevant issues one is undertaking citizenly duties, 'Critical thinking cannot be viewed simply as a form of progressive reasoning; it must be seen as a fundamental, political act' (1981, p. 57). McCall holds that 'The historic connection between reasoning and citizenship highlights *the* role aspect of citizenship. Although we have no verb for it, "citizening" was *taking part* in deliberation' [my italics] (1991, p 37). It is imperative that in taking part one should deliberate, consider, reflect and inquire into one's society or community. Lindfors agrees with this sentiment and stresses that in inquiring we are fulfilling a social function and we should conduct our inquiring with others around us: 'Because we inquire *of others* in order to further our understanding, inquiry is as much a social act as it is an intellectual one' (1999, p. 2).

A question is posed by Faulks (2000),

> Could it be that the concept of citizenship is becoming redundant, since its close association historically with closed political communities is inappropriate to the boundaries of a new global age? ... globalisation appears to challenge the contemporary relevance of citizenship because it blurs the boundaries, both material and psychological, which have made citizenship significant in modernity.
>
> (Faulks, 2000, p. 132)

Moral Citizens

It is precisely the point, that as social animals we *are* involved both in, and *as*, political communities – we *are* responsible for public affairs, for the efficiency with which the machine that is our society runs, for the decisions that are taken which have bearing on the others within and outwith the group, for the consequences that result from our action or passivity. It is our *duty* to become active members of a society in order to generate community. It is important that we strive toward something more than society, more than a collection of individuals living in proximity with one another and interacting in certain ways to provide food, shelter and organization within the group; community is something more. Certainly there are rules that should be kept and still people will need food and shelter, but rather than functioning on an individualistic principle where everyone is concerned with what he or she has for him or herself, individuals work together for some common goal and are aware that what they do should be for the good of everyone as a whole. Thus, one might suggest that the community is the 'I' in this situation and the composite individuals are a range of selves striving to create the 'I' of community, and, as the self ultimately has no choice but to form the 'I', so too if there is commitment to forming a community the members are bound to work toward this. Faulks (2000) suggests that

> Duties may be seen as those responsibilities imposed by law and carry some kind of sanction if the individual does not honour them. Obligations, in contrast, may be seen as voluntary and as an expression of solidarity and empathy with others.
>
> (Faulks, 2000, p. 82)

He continues, 'The mark of a healthy society is its ability to rely upon obligations rather than imposed duties to maintain the conditions of the community' (*ibid.*, p. 82). I would here disagree with Faulks. Certainly duties *may* be seen as responsibilities which are imposed by some external force, however, obligations, it would appear, are moral duties – we are bound morally to act, and act in a way that is of benefit to society. Bearing in mind that citizens are persons, in that they are treating the community as an end in itself and not merely as a means to the individuals' ends and that each person has a moral code then this code is what encourages or motivates the striving for community beyond society where it is possible not to be a citizen and where one may not feel bound by the duties or obligations created within the society. There are, similarly, consequences if one does not carry out one's obligations, although less obvious than the legally enshrined sanctions enforced if one fails to carry out one's duty. For instance, it is an individual's duty to pay certain taxes and if one fails to do so then one will suffer at the hands of the legislative system. If, however, one does not undertake his/her obligation towards other individuals on a personal level, such as in the way one behaves toward them, for example by repeatedly missing work or arriving late to miss appointments, then one will find that the consequence of these actions is that the job will be lost, house repayments cannot be met, and so on. It is in our own interests and the interests of those around us that we adopt and maintain the accepted moral code in order to create community. It is imperative that we involve ourselves in the creation and upkeep of our community, and we do this as citizens. We are therefore morally obliged or bound to participate in the workings of our society. Let us consider how our behaviour – as citizens – within society is structured or regulated.

Mill (1985) claims that

> Though society is not founded on a contract, and though no good purpose is answered by inventing a contract in order to deduce social obligations from it, everyone who receives the protection of society owes a return for the benefit, and the fact of living in society renders it indispensable that each should be bound to observe a certain line of conduct towards the rest.
>
> (Mill, 1985, p. 141)

This idea of one having an obligation to one's society and its constituent members was evident in the *polis* of Athens, as Faulks (2000) shows:

> Obligations generally did not take the form of statutory duties. They were perceived by citizens as opportunities to be virtuous and to serve the community. The institutions of government provided many

opportunities for the exercise of civic virtue and were modelled on the maxim that all citizens should be both ruler and ruled.

(Faulks, 2000, p. 17)

...this resulting in a system that gave all citizens the right and opportunity to speak and vote in political assemblies. It could be argued that in promoting this 'civic virtue' and in encouraging a participative citizenry, corruption was – and could be – avoided within the *polis* – or our present society – and that individuals could not sit back and opt out of the decision-making process by allowing others to take it over. As Faulks states, 'A citizenship based upon groups rather than individuals may well lead to more, not less oppression. We must also remember that groups can themselves be oppressive of their members' (*ibid.*, p. 95). So, it is vital that in being active participants (since we cannot participate through inaction) in a society, we create a community and in a community it is hoped that an egalitarian sense of purpose will be engendered. The purpose is itself to create and maintain the community, as within the understanding of community there is a positive attribution; a community is created by and for its members, and works by protecting and providing for its members. It is perfectly feasible that society is composed of a range of communities, but communities are not constituted by smaller societies. Again I would agree with Faulks that 'Citizenship is a status that mediates the relationship between the individual and the political community. Citizenship also provides a framework for the interactions between individuals within civil society' (*ibid.*, p. 107). It should perhaps be noted that while Faulks talks of a 'political community', it might be suggested that in talking of community – which is necessarily made up of citizens who work for the interests of the whole – that community is itself political and Faulks' use of the term 'political' in this instance is somewhat redundant.

Certainly, there is no citizenship without the individual, but then, there is no society in which to take part without individual constituent members – however the members must work together and not necessarily in accordance with one another's views. It cannot be the case that people share the same views, but they do share the common goal that they want the best for their society, and this may vary from group to group, but ultimately an agreement for governance will be reached. Plato (1987a) shares this notion,

> The object of our legislation ... is not the special welfare of any particular class in our society, but of the society as a whole; and it uses persuasion or compulsion to unite all citizens and make them share together the benefits which each individually can confer on the community; and its purpose in fostering this attitude is not to leave everyone to please himself, but to make each man a link in the unity of the whole.
>
> (Plato, 1987a, p. 263)

Acting Citizens

Rousseau correctly highlights the case that 'An individual may be a devout priest, a brave soldier, or a zealous senator, and yet a bad citizen' (1973, p. 133). One is not a 'bad citizen' if one is not participating; in this instance one is not a citizen *at all* since in being a citizen we are required to act. No, a bad citizen is an individual whose aims or motivations are less than those which might be of good or benefit to the community. We are required to act, we are required to make decisions, we are required to participate in our society – we have a duty to create a community, an entity whose constituent parts live together to provide the best for each of its members. Mill states that 'A person may cause evil to others not only by his actions but by his inaction, and in either case he is justly accountable to them for the injury' (1985, p. 70). He continues,

> ... it would be absurd to pretend that people ought to live as if nothing whatever had been known in the world before they came into it; as if experience had as yet done nothing towards showing that one mode of existence, or of conduct, is preferable to another. Nobody denies that people should be taught and trained in youth as to know and benefit by the ascertained results of human experience. But it is

the privilege and proper condition of a human being, arrived at the maturity of his faculties, to use and interpret experience in his own way.

(*ibid.*, p. 122)

But how is this experience to be used? How should this reflective human being manifest his/her convictions? Perhaps Rousseau has a valid point when he suggests that 'To live without doing some good is a great evil as well in the political as in the moral world; and hence every useless citizen should be regarded as a pernicious person' (1973, p. 16). We must, however, add that the political world is the moral world, for our actions as citizens are political actions and ultimately are moral in that they have consequences as a result of their being performed. MacMurray comments along similar lines, 'If we call the harmonious interrelation of agents their "community", we may say that a morally right action is an action which intends community' (1970, p. 119). The idea, then, is that we, as individual citizens, should strive for the greatest good for the community and the most advantageous way we have of ensuring this is to enshrine our duties and responsibilities in formal rules and legislation. In other words, we legalize the majority moral code in order that everyone is aware of what is expected of and from them or what is unacceptable behaviour or conduct within a certain society or community; as Downie suggests '... rules are concerned with organizing *group* interests' (1971, p. 35).

Rousseau (1973) claims that

Apart from the primitive contract, the vote of the majority always binds the rest. This follows from the contract itself. But it is asked how a man can be both free and forced to conform to wills that are not his own. How are the opponents at once free and subject to laws they have not agreed to? I retort that the question is wrongly put. The citizen gives his consent to all the laws, including those which punish him when he dares to break any of them. The constant will of all the members of the State is the general will; by virtue of it they are citizens and free.

(Rousseau, 1973, p. 277)

This links closely to the earlier point that the moral code of the majority takes on the mantle of policy shaping. Rousseau's *Social Contract* builds on this, '. . . each individual, as a man, may have a particular will contrary or dissimilar to the general will which he has as a citizen' (*ibid.*, p. 194). As a citizen one is adopting another role, one which lacks self-interest and is keen to work for the good of the community. Indeed, Faulks echoes the point that without different moral codes there would be no disagreement, or rather, disagreement occurs precisely because there is a sense of defending one's moral code to those who hold differing codes: 'Without diversity and conflicts of interests, we would have no need for politics' (2000, p. 100). We must, however, be careful that in creating rules and regulations for the society to live *by* (rather than live *under*) we do not create some kind of dictatorship; the people as decision makers is crucial. Faulks highlights a positive aspect to citizenship when he says that 'The advantage citizenship has over other social identities is that it has an inclusive quality that other identities such as class, religion or ethnicity lack' (*ibid.*, p. 107), thus we must strive to create the most inclusive society possible while not ignoring or denying difference. By allowing that individuals are autonomous agents we facilitate active citizenry.

One way individuals have been empowered to exercise their citizenship is by the means of participating in citizens' juries. Rather than a focus group whose opinions are sought – after a sample of voters has been canvassed – citizens' juries give individuals the opportunity to take an active role in decision-making. Faulks highlights that

> While there are clearly dangers with allowing public policy to be shaped only by those directly affected by a particular decision, the experience of such [citizens'] juries has been encouraging in that participants experience a sense of empowerment that is often lacking in minimalist models of participation such as voting. Citizens' juries have also produced well-considered and insightful policy suggestions.
>
> (*ibid.*, p. 113)

As voter apathy is on the increase in Britain, coupled with the fact that voting is not a particularly participative or representative activity, then the idea of citizens' juries may be one worth considering in order that individuals are able to become more involved and active and truly be citizens. This form of community service, that is, doing a service for one's community, would breed the egalitarian nature and interdependent spirit required to be a true and effective citizenship. Some may argue that all members of a society should at some stage contribute to their living environment by taking some formally required period of time to engage in community service, be that cleaning the streets, visiting the elderly, planting trees or working with charitable organizations. This then falls back into the realms of the duty or obligation argument. However, there is a reciprocal arrangement, and this is perhaps what the individuals should offer – time and skills – in conjunction with living according to the established rules. As Faulks says, 'Community is the structural context of individual agency and as such it is hardly unreasonable to expect all citizens to take some responsibility for its maintenance' (*ibid.*, p. 115).

Emmet (1966) questions our motives for using our moral codes to determine the behaviour of others:

> Is there any satisfactory reason why they [our principles] should be 'really right' even for us? And even if so, is there any justification for our trying to press them on other people in moral criticism or moral advice? Or is morality rather a prudential matter, a way of calculating what behaviour is most likely to conduce favourable consequences to ourselves and others?
>
> (Emmet, 1966, p. 1)

Emmet appears to have answered her own question. She has provided the justification she was looking for in imposing a moral code on others; the justification *is* that it is conducive to positive behaviours towards ourselves and others. Personhood, therefore, is maintained. In order to communicate, cooperate and live within a community it is reasonable to expect that we abide by parameters of behaviour agreed by the group, but established by the moral majority code – it does not necessarily imply that we act as automatons with one mode of being and dare not deviate. There is always something rather constructed about the way we behave or interact with others within our sphere; as Emmet suggests

> ... social behaviour is always artificial, in the sense that it is not just unlearned or impulsive. It is informed by expectations to which people have been taught to conform, as to how they should behave in certain relationships and situations; this may come to seem 'natural' where the expectations are so strongly grounded in custom and so widely accepted that they have come to seem self-evident.
>
> (*ibid.*, p. 40)

This socialization begins at a very young age, in fact, immediately one is born, in order that custom is 'naturalized' as quickly as possible to facilitate the growing into society. Elkin and Handel's definition of socialization is a useful one: 'Socialization may be defined as *the process by which we learn the ways of a given society or social group so that we can function within it*' (1978, p. 4). Rules are set to promote the interests of the people that form the society – even in the wider global context. When a situation arises we do not think through the whole situation. For example, if the opportunity presented itself that a handbag was lying open beside someone's chair and the purse inside was clearly visible and accessible, I do not deliberate over the taking of the purse each time – I am aware of the rules of my society, those that are formally legislated and those that are implicitly agreed by the members of that society. It has already been argued that individuals do not necessarily hold the same moral code, however, even if my moral code were different to the rule that I should not take things that do not belong to me, I would be bound not to if, in fact, I desired to remain within the society or community and wished to retain my personhood. This allows, then, that there are not necessarily any universal moral rules, but that context plays its part and societal rules *may* alter with a change in governmental policy decided by the new majority moral code or in the event of a situation which prompted the breaking of the code; for example, if one were acting in self-defence or if one was responsible for feeding one's children and had no money and opted to 'steal' from the local supermarket in order that the children receive some nourishment, context cannot be ignored.

Indeed, killing is often not perceived as being wrong if the country is at war. Emmet (1966) is correct to assert that

> Ethics and sociology are indeed distinct, 'situation' is not just a conjunction of circumstances, but a conjunction of circumstances including social relationships seen as a unity in reference to actual or prospective action or interests, or to the attitudes of human beings.
>
> (Emmet, 1966, p. 138)

Rousseau's introduction to his *Social Contract* hints at his feeling that there is an agreed mode of behaviour:

> We no longer dare seem what we really are, but lie under perpetual restraint; in the meantime the herd of men, which we call society, all act under the same circumstances alike, unless very particular and powerful motives prevent them.
>
> (Rousseau, 1973, p. 6)

This also suggests that Rousseau believes there to be some social role, that we consciously play a part, or at least accept a part, that allows us to integrate with the others in society in order that it may function effectively. It is clear, from Emmet, that in wanting to be part of the society – by accepting our role, and in adopting this role – we must abide by the appended rules of that role within that society:

> ... to say someone has a certain role does not *explain* his behaviour unless it is being understood that he accepts this role so that it provides premises for his decisions. There may be 'social pressures' on him to act as is expected in his role: but 'social pressures' are not physical forces; they are ways of providing people with strong motives for doing one thing rather than another.
>
> (Emmet, 1966, p. 126)

Having said that one adopts, or agrees to adopt, the role given by society, it is not necessarily the case that one must adopt the citizen role; one can have a position in society without being active in the sense that one strives for the good of others within the group. However, one may incidentally work for the benefit of others without the actual desire to do so by perhaps the occupation one has. This is similar in kind to the argument that one may be a person in that one performs 'personly' tasks or activities almost by accident, or at least not deliberately. One must wonder, though, what incentive one has to take on the citizen role if ultimately one will reap the benefits of someone else's labour. Rousseau (1973), in a somewhat jocular and impracticable manner, asserts how important it is that citizens should best be involved in the structuring of their society,

> I should have sought a country {to be born in}, in which the right legislation was vested in all the citizens; for who can judge better than they of the conditions under which they had best dwell together in the same society.
>
> (Rousseau, 1973, p. 35)

He goes on to strike some sort of balance between the idea of looking out for the interest of the community without abdicating a sense of self-interest, rather than living by the 'Golden Rule' of doing to others as you would have them do to you. He suggests that we should, instead, be inspired by '... that other maxim of natural goodness, much less perfect indeed, but perhaps more useful; *Do good to yourself with as little evil as possible to others*' (*ibid.*, p. 76).

Rousseau builds on the idea that in becoming a part of society, there is some need to regulate the behaviour we may naturally possess as part of our 'animal' moral code. He states that

> Morality began to appear in human actions, and everyone, before the institution of law, was the only judge and avenger of the injuries done him, so that the goodness which was suitable in the pure state of nature was no longer proper in the new-born state of society.
>
> (*ibid.*, p. 91)

Lawson stresses this point stating that 'The contract of mutual obligations refers not only to the relationships between individuals and the state but also to the relationships between individuals' (2001, p. 169). Within his *Social Contract* Rousseau is eager to establish that we have no authority – naturally – over others and that it is custom or convention that forms the authority under which we reside. Indeed, even the voting system present within our society has been instituted and established as a result of convention, as Rousseau indicates, 'Laws are, properly speaking, only the conditions of civil association' (1973, p. 212). He goes on to suggest the point made earlier, that the majority moral code is in power and adds that a society can be assessed as a result of this; '. . . the way in which general business is managed may give a clear enough indication of the actual state of morals and health of the body politic' (*ibid.*, p. 276). We, therefore, in assenting to abide by the majority moral code – although there is the facility for the demotion of the powerful and decision-making party – are agreeing to live by the rules laid down in legislation. Emmet does point out that '. . . change may not be met in a way which makes for the development of morality itself' (1966, p. 105). However, it is necessary, in order that society does not collapse, to work within the structural confines of the electoral system available to us in our Western society. It does not mean, however, that if society were to collapse that community would also. Perhaps we are, in fact, perpetuating a society that is not to our mutual benefit, but should concentrate on creating and maintaining a community with an active citizenry as its members. Mill (1985) indicates that there is little more than our personal preference that encourages the way we elect our governors; in *On Liberty* he states that it is

The likings and dislikings of society, or of some powerful portion of it, [that] are thus the main thing which has practically determined the rules laid down for general observance . . . People decide according to their personal preferences.

(Mill, 1985, p. 67)

Reciprocal Citizens

It was earlier stated, however, that there is a reciprocal arrangement in place with regard to being a citizen; so in return for practising good citizen behaviour, let us now examine what citizens gain from the State – other than the satisfaction of being a citizen within a community, though some may hold this to be sufficient. Faulks suggests that 'As well as having the opportunity and the responsibility to participate politically, citizens also require the resources to enable them to participate. The community has a duty to provide for every citizen's basic needs' (2000, p. 116).

These 'basic needs' are often translated into what are commonly perceived of as *rights*. In being given authority or permission to rule, the State must provide the most basic of rights – some form of security for its citizens. This security may manifest itself in a set of laws or rules which protect individuals or groups physically; these laws do not necessarily stop someone murdering another individual, but if not deterred from committing the 'crime', the murderer will be liable to face the legal consequences, for instance, imprisonment in this country, the death penalty in others. 'Penalty' being a useful term to describe what is incurred in breaking an agreed rule. Rights, or security, may also be provided in the forms of food and shelter. Our physical wellbeing must be protected – and nurtured – if we are to perform expected duties/obligations as part of being an effective citizen. Some governments may instil some form of *social* security in the form of monetary payments, for example, income support, housing benefit, disability living allowance. The titles of these monetary payments are certainly no coincidence – 'support', 'benefit', 'allowance'. They, the governments, may also provide free education and a public health service. In *Citizenship* Faulks posits that 'Our individual rights are only meaningful when they are supported by a sense of obligation amongst others both to recognise our rights and to help us build and sustain the social institutions that make rights possible' (2000, p. 164).

This is where the difference between State and Government is evident. Government legislates for these rights, it finances the institutions which cater for our needs and enables us to access our rights and entitlements. The State – in some ways – remains constant while Governments and their policies may change. It is the mechanism that facilitates the needs, rights, entitlements; schools, hospitals, the emergency services and job centres are all institutions founded within the State. One may go further and suggest that such things as these *are* the State, with citizens working within it to put into action what the organizations/institutions have been established for.

There is a link here to what Faulks earlier called the 'political community'. Government is political by its very nature and we, as politically active, voting (or dissenting) citizens, depend upon the political community with the power to provide for these rights. Further, in working for these rights we should exercise them, especially, as Faulks maintains, '... where these rights are fundamental to the good of the community' (*ibid.*, p. 108). It is our responsibility to participate – and generate participation – with and for the political community, he says, 'It is an ethic of participation ... that is the key to uniting rights and responsibilities as reciprocal ideas' (*ibid.*, p. 106). Rousseau indicates that once one has 'established' a citizenry we must do more than protect its members; '... it is also necessary to consider their substance' (1973, p. 151). While the monetary payments provided by the Government through State institutions are available in this country, they tend, in the main, to be available to those suffering from some form of hardship or difficulty, for example unemployment, age, and so on. However, Faulks highlights an idea that may actively engender citizenship within society as a step towards community – that of the Citizens' Income (CI).

'CI sometimes referred to as basic income, is a guaranteed sum of money paid to each adult citizen (with perhaps a lower rate for children) regardless of their employment status' (2000, p. 119). It could be argued that in providing a Citizens' Income the reciprocal nature of the relationship between the State and its individual members is valued – the citizen and his/her needs are placed above market needs. This financial arrangement would inevitably feed back into the larger system, while being of benefit to individual constituent members in that voluntary work (community service), lifelong learning and political participation would be returned. Being a citizen in this instance would be almost like taking a job of work and receiving payment; there would be a contract in the sense that one would be expected to perform certain citizenry duties, yet, one would have a sense of value and purpose in working for the betterment of all – including oneself – within the community. It may also be worthy of consideration that the notion of *voluntary* work must come into question if it is a duty or obligation on which payments depends. It is not to be ignored that this motivating factor towards an active and participatory citizenship and citizenry appears, in this light, to be of little intrinsic value and that individuals are almost being bribed to be active in their communities which would run counter to the idea of a positive community of citizens. What is to be hoped is that the CI is seen as a reward more than an incentive to play a role in one's society in trying to create a community.

It is important to recognize that while we are citizens striving for some common good in the shape of community, this citizenry is constituted of *individuals*, and it cannot be forgotten that we are individuals before we are able to be citizens by virtue of nature. Rousseau (1973) emphasizes this point when he asks

> ... does not the undertaking entered into by the whole body of the nation bind it to provide for the security of the least of its members with as much care as for that of all the rest? Is the welfare of a single citizen any less the common cause than that of the whole State? It may be said that it is good that one should perish for all.
>
> (Rousseau, 1973, p. 144)

Certainly we, as individuals, are entitled to provision and protection by the State or smaller community, and in affording individuals these rights then individual autonomy is being acknowledged. Yes, we are part of a greater 'machine', but equally, we are capable of self-government and self-regulation; if this were not the case, there would be no place for democracy. Rights, in and of themselves, are not natural, we were not born 'into the woods' possessing rights or entitlements. It is through the founding of societies and social interactions that the need for rights rises to the surface. In agreeing to abide by the rules or laws of the society in which we live, we are taking on the inherent duties or obligations, and in participating in such a manner, rights, or the need for rights, occur as a consequence. Rights and obligations/duties go hand in hand; they are mutually dependent in order that a reciprocal arrangement may be formed between a society and its members in generating a community for its citizens. Further, while this implies some form of contract, one should be aware that a contract tends to be static, yet there is some kind of agreement between the parties concerned in the setting up of rights and responsibilities, and this agreement can at times be flexible or even change direction altogether. Faulks suggests that in order to encourage individuals to take on responsibilities and to ensure that those more vulnerable members of society do not have their rights impinged upon, is '... to approach citizenship more holistically and to see rights and responsibilities not as intrinsically opposed, but as mutually supportive' (2000, p. 73). One might say in order that the rights we 'enjoy' be maintained, we must accept that in order to sustain the community, we have to take on responsibilities. However, it could also be suggested that it is our responsibility to build a community from our society, and in doing thus, we are then entitled to certain rights.

McCall (1991) posits the following:

> In order for a democracy to work, it is not enough to merely allow a vote to everyone. An effective democracy requires effective citizens, people who are active in the organisation of their own lives and in their society. But to be active and effective as a citizen, a person must be able to think critically, to weigh different alternatives, to evaluate reasons given for particular decisions or policies which affect the community. To be an active and effective citizen requires both the disposition to reason and the skills required for effective reasoning.
>
> (McCall, 1991, p. 2)

It is, of course, true that we would each rather that everyone wanted the same as us, whether in terms of how we live or in how we relate and interact with one another. However, as humans with our own individual moral code, this cannot be the case. As Mill (1985) states,

> ... an opinion on a point of conduct, not supported by reasons, can only count as one person's preference; and if the reasons, when given, are a mere appeal to a similar preference felt by other people, it is still only many people's liking instead of one.
>
> (Mill, 1985, p. 64)

It is necessary, however, that opinions are shared and discussed; necessary, in the first place, that everyone is valued as an individual, contributing member to the community and necessary, also, in order that the community can make the most informed decision about the way forward. Mill suggests that 'If all mankind minus one were of one opinion, mankind would be no more justified in silencing that one person than he, if he had the power, would be justified in silencing mankind' (*ibid.*, p. 76). If we were to silence the view of the minority we cannot predict the potential harm we could be doing to our society. We could not even avail ourselves of the excuse that our actions were morally right, for even if we could be certain that the suppressed opinion was false, we cannot disregard our neighbours if we are to be true citizens striving to maintain an inclusive community. Further, one cannot predict either when one may be in the minority and feel the need for an opinion to be listened to. Additionally, it is nowhere implied that the expression of an opinion must necessitate the suggested action – 'No one pretends that actions should be as free as opinions,' (*ibid.*, p. 119) asserts Mill. However, it is not sufficient to offer an opinion; there must be some form of dialogue or discussion in order that effective action can be undertaken.

Emmet (1966) is keen to highlight that

> Rational behaviour is not of course the same as ethical behaviour; it may be concerned with questions of policy, interest, advantage, which are not directly ethical (though in a context of complex human

relations these may well have ethical implications and there may indeed be a moral obligation to take account of them).

(Emmet, 1966, p. 188)

One may go further and say that *all* decisions *will* have ethical implications on individuals, and it is our duty, our responsibility, to take account of how our decisions affect those others within our society. And they are *our* decisions, even if it is only by dint of our putting in place a group of people (a government) to enforce or legislate for the things we as individuals believe in. It is worth highlighting the 2003 declaration of war on Iraq and the huge protests against such action around the world. This is a useful example of an elected government following a course of action that failed to satisfy the moral codes of a very large proportion of society; this opposing group took action to register their dissent. While this group may not be in favour of the war, the members of the group are still bound to take account of how the government's actions impact on other individuals – even if they state clearly 'Not in my name'.

It is true that things such as focus groups or citizens' juries take time to establish and more time to discuss the issues relating to our lives as individuals or as a group, and the lives of those perhaps not within our direct social sphere, for instance in terms of international relations. It might be suggested, though, that in having an open and accessible forum for discussion and opinion/idea sharing, that more people would become interested in becoming involved in the process. It would have to be said that this system would be a transparent one, one where citizens would be able to see the process through from beginning to end – an open system where information is shared, where citizens can see the effects of their discussions. While these discussions are necessary, there needs to be something more, something deeper; it is not enough to assert an opinion or point of view – one must reason with the others in the society or community.

Conclusions

So, in this chapter we have seen that for one to be a citizen one should participate in the running of one's society or community, and one cannot participate by being inactive. There is some form of reciprocity built into the notion of citizenship; in order to gain the benefits of being a citizen one must acknowledge that it is a role and as such there are duties or responsibilities bound up in this. One is called, in being a citizen to be political, political in the sense that one takes an interest in and works for the betterment of the society. Of course the majority moral code impacts on what is considered the 'right' or better thing for society, but in being active and political citizens we are able to work for what is collectively agreed – bearing in mind that in being a person and in being a citizen, one has agreed to abide by the majority moral code. One of the ways individual citizens can air their agreement or disagreement with the running of the society was raised – that of the citizens' jury. While voting in general elections allows minimal participation, it has been suggested here that citizens' juries may be one way of promoting citizen involvement. At the end of the chapter it was suggested that in order for a democracy to be effective its citizens should not only be encouraged to be involved, but also that they should be expected to think and reflect critically in their citizen role; and this is what will be discussed in the following chapter.

7

Community of Philosophical
Inquiry: A Tool for Empowerment

In Chapter 6 the idea of being a critical and reflective citizen was introduced; in this chapter one model for promoting this type of participation will be considered – the practice of Community of Philosophical Inquiry. This practice is egalitarian in nature and promotes in its structure the idea of working for a common goal or purpose. The practice does not allow for status and over time the participants will grow into a community where dialogue is seen as more important than the individual and constituent members. The community inquires on a deep and philosophical level and it will be posited that this would be a powerful and effective model along which lines citizens' juries could be run. The crucial role of the Facilitator of the Philosophical Inquiry will be considered and linked also to Socrates' role in ancient Athens in the bringing to birth the ideas of those engaged in dialogue. It will be suggested that to be a truly effective citizen one must be able to reason critically and effectively.

Reasoning Citizens

In reasoning one is truly inquiring into a subject; the group involved is looking for alternative viewpoints and perspectives on which to build for the betterment of all concerned. As McCall (1991) holds,

> If we understand the nature of citizenship to be that of active parti-
> cipation in the community and an effective citizen to be a person who
> affects what happens in their community, then what it means to be an
> effective citizen will involve inquiry and reasoning.
>
> (McCall, 1991, p. 39)

She also maintains that 'People are capable of reasoning by virtue of being human beings, but to be proficient takes practice' (*ibid.*, p. 38). It is clear that in ancient Athens the citizens were encouraged to participate in policy making (with the exclusion of women and slaves). Indeed, being able to deliberate with others as an equal was a *right*. Status within the male community of the *polis* was not of any importance at these meetings. In fact, McCall suggests that

> The egalitarian assumptions, under which all citizens (though not all
> people) had an equal right to participate in self government, led to a
> structure under which public argumentation, whether deliberation or
> persuasion, produced joint decision making either by consensus or
> vote.
>
> (*ibid.*, p. 37)

In thus involving individuals in the decision-making process and in seeking differing opinions, it means that there is the potential for all views to be considered. Further, McCall adds that

> ... to be a good citizen – to be willing and able to reason with others –
> commits a person to regard others as equals ... So one cannot be a
> good citizen and simultaneously regard, for example, women as being
> unequal to men.
>
> (*ibid.*, p. 37)

It is important, also, that one's reasoning, one's assumptions should be challenged or questioned in order that the 'correct' decisions can be made and that there is understanding from where decisions have come. In respecting the ideas of others, one will in turn, it is hoped,

demonstrate tolerance of other opinions and decisions reached
which have been influenced by dialogue with various citizens,
while also being tolerant of and respectful towards those taking
part in the discussions – that is, those other citizens around us. We
should, McCall maintains, also be aware that 'Considering all
people as potential contributors to one's reasoning has very strong
egalitarian implications' (*ibid.*, p. 31); again we are back in the *polis*
of Athens where status is disregarded and ideas and the sharing of
opinions are what count towards generating a community with an
active and participatory citizenry.

McCall is not alone in her thinking that communities should be
governed by the decisions of the citizens after reasoning dialogue
has taken place with its constituent members. However, it is Plato
that introduces the suggestion that it is philosophers, or those who
philosophize – reason – who are rulers. Plato (1987a) holds that the
desired society

> ... can never grow into a reality or see the light of day, and there will
> be no end to the troubles of states, or indeed, ... of humanity itself,
> till philosophers become kings in this world, or till those we now call
> kings and rulers really and truly become philosophers, and political
> power and philosophy thus come into the same hands.
>
> (Plato, 1987a, p. 202)

Adeimantus interrupts within the dialogue to assert what many
have said since, that those who truly study philosophy are odd and
eventually are '... reduced ... to complete uselessness as members
of society' (*ibid.*, p. 221). It may be said that the *study of* philosophy
leads one to be less than active within society, however, if one
practises the skills inherent in philosophy and philosophical dialogue, the merits can be seen. Indeed, in her *Stevenson Lectures on
Citizenship*, McCall discusses the need for a reasoning citizenry if we
require a democracy, and goes on to highlight that – contrary to
Plato's notion that we should study philosophy – we should be
reasoning citizens. Reasoning, though, is not something we are
actively encouraged to practise, and like any other skill, in order to
reason proficiently one requires practise. McCall (1991) states

clearly the prerequisite for being a reasoning, reflective and effective citizen,

> ... a person needs to be able to make reasoned judgements concerning the views of others, and needs to be able to modify his or her view if necessary. This requires comprehension skills, which in turn requires skill in analogical reasoning as well as in recognising and evaluating analogies; identifying assumptions; recognising fallacies; being careful about jumping to conclusions; recognising part/whole relationships; always being aware of alternatives; seeking out consistencies and inconsistencies in every sphere of life.
>
> (McCall, 1991, p. 2)

So, how could society encourage or facilitate this reasoning among individuals? Certainly citizens' juries would be a very useful means of gathering individuals together, but how would – or could – their discussions be facilitated? McCall has developed a practice which could potentially function as a means to creating reasoned dialogue in order that policy-making decisions take account of a wide range of opinions and ideas – the practice of Community of Philosophical Inquiry (COPI).

Community of Philosophical Inquiry

It is essential, first, that the practice of COPI is described in some detail. Community of Philosophical Inquiry takes place with a group of approximately, and ideally, 12 participants. All participants are present on an equal footing, status is not, indeed *cannot*, be present. The notion of all being equal is evident in the seating arrangements – the participants sit in a circle and are equidistant to their neighbours in the circle, thus no one is set apart as some kind of authority figure – or as someone whose ideas are to be disregarded. Also, by placing the seats in this manner each member of the group is able to see each participant clearly. There is an anonymity rule within COPI whereby one need not use one's real name or give any details or information regarding one's personal life. In so doing, certain assumptions can be discarded or avoided and individuals are free to engage in the inquiry itself. For instance, if Professor Farquhar Whatley-Smythe of City University, and Mary Jones the assembly-line worker, were in the same group it is perfectly feasible that either they, or others within the group would make unnecessary assumptions about these individuals which may impinge upon their behaviour, and ultimately the dialogue. As McCall rightly holds,

> ...the egalitarianism assumed by the Community of Philosophical Inquiry, and the egalitarianism assumed by democratic forms of organisation do not imply that every person is the same. It does imply that all people have the potential to put forward ideas and arguments which have not been foreseen by others, and also that all people no matter how brilliant or knowledgeable are fallible.
>
> (*ibid.*, p. 37)

This links to the three main assumptions that underlie the practice of Community of Philosophical Inquiry; first, that as human beings we all have the disposition and capacity to reason; secondly, we are all fallible – as humans – and thirdly, we are all creative beings. In saying that as humans we are creative, one is simply stating that we are '... capable of generating original ideas. This does not mean that every person does in fact originate new ideas, but that by virtue of the fact that an individual is a human being, any individual has creative potential' (*ibid.*, p. 30).

In suggesting that we have the disposition to reason implies that not only do we have the capacity to reason, but also we are *able* to reason interactively with other members of the Community. McCall would argue

> ...that it is not just coincidence that the COPI, which requires certain kinds of behaviour from its members, simultaneously induces reasoning skills. The disposition to reason with others, which involves behavioural skills of listening, relating one's thoughts to those of others, taking into account other points of view and alternatives, etc., cannot be effectively actualised without using reasoning skills.
>
> (*ibid.*, p. 26)

Not only are we reasoning beings, but this reasoning comes partly as a result of our creativity and partly our creativity is evidenced through our reasoning. McCall is clear that this creative part of our make-up plays an essential role within the COPI – and therefore within the wider world. She claims that none

> ...of the features of the western model of rationality make allowance for another feature of human nature which is crucial to reasoning – that people are creative. Reasoning, whether taken as private ratiocination, or as public argumentation, requires creativity. Although it may have been made by others in the past, the first time an individual puts forward an argument, he must innovate. He has to meet objections, interpret evidence and make connections between elements in the situation which had not previously been coordinated.
>
> (*ibid.*, p. 29)

Linked strongly to this creative and reasoning aspect of human nature and the COPI is the fact that, as humans, we are all fallible.

> If there were such a thing as infallible human beings there would be no need to engage in philosophical dialogue in order to inquire. But if there were such things as infallible human beings, any form of democracy would be an inefficient way to organise society and effective membership, or rather effective membership of such a society would require very different forms of behaviour than the kinds required for effective citizenship within a democracy.
>
> (*ibid.*, p. 23)

This notion of fallibility is essential to the egalitarian process engendered by Community of Philosophical Inquiry.

Philosophical Citizens

It is necessary for an effective citizen to be able to act; however, one must not act 'blindly'. In order that action is effected in an appropriate manner for the betterment of the society or community, then thinking and reasoning skills must be utilized. One must be prepared to counter opposition in a reasoned and properly calculated manner. COPI models this by using a structure that remains constant with each group. After reading a shared text and offering questions to the Facilitator of the inquiry, participants are expected to agree or disagree with previous statements while also giving reasons for that agreement or disagreement. Consensus or absolute conclusions are not drawn from inquiry, rather the format and structure allow for the examination of assumptions that underlie or underpin the concepts that are often accepted unquestioningly within our societal structures. McCall holds that

> The dialogue procedure requires members of the community [COPI] to listen to the ideas and arguments of others, to make explicit the relationship between viewpoints or arguments being presented, to present arguments and counter-arguments, to give reasons, to evaluate the reasons given.

> (*ibid.*, p. 18)

So, what initially was a group of individuals discussing issues raised from 'jump off' questions becomes an active and participative community engaged in philosophical dialogue. And this community has, as its common purpose or goal, the desire to inquire together, to generate a dialogue and search for deeper meanings which challenge the assumptions held within the community. This is where and when the community is formed, this is its common purpose – the philosophical dialogue. Similar to the citizens' juries, which meet for up to five consecutive days, these Communities of Philosophical Inquiry meet regularly in order to establish a 'working' relationship – a community. Very often within a COPI participants know little or nothing of the other members' lives; they discuss philosophical issues, examine assumptions and generate ideas without the need (and often the desire) to know personal details. This is useful to both the participants and the dialogue in that interaction is uncluttered with personal 'baggage', agendas or assumptions, no matter how accurate those assumptions may be. Citizens' juries could be modelled along a similar line; groups would meet regularly, formed randomly by people within society to discuss and focus on the issues under inquiry. There are obvious logistical issues such as participants needing to live fairly close to one another, which *may* have the implication that the juries or groups or communities are composed almost entirely of one section of society – perhaps there may be difficulties, too, in more rural areas. It is certainly not the case, however, that individuals think in the same way or hold the same opinions or philosophical assumptions purely on account of their geographical backgrounds.

In discussing the practice of COPI, McCall (1991) highlights that

> ... the important feature of Philosophical Inquiry is that kinds of thinking and behaviour which are not rational, *cannot* succeed. It is through engaging in dialogue that participants come to know what succeeds in furthering the inquiry. They discover for themselves that certain kinds of thinking and interaction do not further the inquiry.
>
> (McCall, 1991, p. 18)

This perhaps begs the question that in participating in a COPI over time, would a participant's behaviour and thinking *outwith* the small community be changed in the wider society, thus working towards forming a larger community from the society in which the COPI or citizens' jury is placed? Certainly, it may be claimed – and has been anecdotally – that individual behaviours and thinking have been altered for the better by those who have undertaken the practice of COPI over a period of time. For instance, a group of women from an economically deprived area within Glasgow who had undertaken a series of COPI sessions were given the impetus and confidence to form another group, a pressure group, to approach the City Council and fight to be allowed to make environmentally friendly changes to their housing. Others suggest a sense of positive self-image has been generated and an increase in confidence in dealing with difficult employers, and there have been those who feel they are able to express their thoughts and ideas more clearly and articulately in order to defend a position in light of opposition from an authority figure. Lipman asserts that when practical philosophy is encountered 'There is a familiar ripple effect outward, like the stone thrown in the pond: wider and wider, more and more encompassing communities are formed' (1988, p. 20). As a small group, or community, formed as a result of participating in a COPI, others are infected by the sense of enablement and become equally empowered either in personal terms or towards their various communities.

Further to presenting arguments and counter arguments, examining assumptions and offering examples to illustrate points raised, the participants have a 'common' language. Within COPI no one is permitted to make direct reference to an 'authority' or source to back up their arguments; it is the community's thinking and reasoning that is important – bearing in mind that if, indeed, all are fallible, then so too is the 'authority', thus leaving *everything* open to question for the COPI. It is also part of the structure of COPI that individuals may not use technical language or jargon. For instance, a computer operator or plumber or doctor or philosopher will have access to terminology that others in the group may not, and in order that everyone understands the ideas being put forward, they must be as clear as possible. Clarity should not be confused with a lack of complexity. Similarly, there are words in every day usage which – in a philosophical context – carry potentially different meanings, and therefore understandings. For example, one may refer to one's self or other persons or of being conscious of something, however, these notions carry with them many assumptions that would need to be unpacked. MacMurray favours this idea of people speaking in a common language with as little ambiguity as possible; he holds that 'The effective medium of philosophical language is ordinary speech at its richest, used with precision' (1970, p. 18). It is in striving to say what one means and mean what one says that creates some kind of clarity and shared meaning in the Community of Philosophical Inquiry.

This idea of a 'common' language is another equalizing tool within the practice of COPI which could work well within citizens' juries to facilitate dialogue and ultimately understanding in order to move society further towards community. In offering ideas to the community within COPI one does not have to posit one's own personally held beliefs or opinions. Indeed, it is important that all are aware that this is the case and that the group, in growing towards a community, equally become aware that they as individuals become less important and that it is, in fact, the ideas within the dialogue that are important. McCall (1991) explains.

> The Community of Philosophical Inquiry does not operate like a spell checker, rather it allows for the recognition of human fallibility on the part of participants, which in turn allows the individual to follow the dialogue, to inquire into the subject unfettered by the need to defend the correctness of their own views.
>
> (McCall, 1991, p. 22)

There is, in fact, no need to express one's *own* view; the individuals as entities cease to be important in the sense that there is no leader in the group, there is no status afforded to any member and it is necessary that the constituent members cooperate and work together,

> ...the COPI involves more than just the use of philosophical reasoning to pursue philosophical questions. It is created by participants engaging in philosophical dialogue in order to pursue a *joint* inquiry. Individuals within a COPI do not compete with each other, but rather contribute to the inquiry being undertaken by the group.
>
> (*ibid.*, p. 19)

and in turn, work toward their common goal. While a COPI does not search for a consensus or for definitive answers, the structure could easily be translated for citizens' juries and what arises in the dialogues could be put to use in decision and policy-making for the wider community. It is essential that an issue be looked at from as many aspects as is possible before policy or legislation is made. It may even prove to be the case that if citizens were encouraged to be part of citizens' juries in the form of a COPI, that much less formal policy and legislation would need to be made since a more positive relationship between and among citizens would evolve. Mill (1985) recognized the value inherent in sharing ideas and opinions and in listening to the views of others and in being influenced by what one has heard:

> Ninety-nine in a hundred are what are called educated men in this condition, even those who can argue fluently for their opinions. Their conclusions may be true, but it might be false for anything they know; they have never thrown themselves into the mental position of those who think differently from them, and considered what such persons may have to say; and, consequently, they do not, in any proper sense of the word, know the doctrine which they themselves profess.
>
> (Mill, 1985, p. 99)

In addition to the fact that all ideas/opinions are shared, the fact that no consensus is reached should be a situation that is clearly mirrored in society. We, as individuals, do not all agree, however, we can and should contribute to the decision-making process – this is part of the reciprocal agreement under which citizens live – this could work within our jury or COPI to demonstrate our alternative ideas, thus potentially facilitating a change in societal policies or regulations/legislations.

Facilitating Citizenship

While COPI is a practice of equals, there is one figure involved who does not participate in the actual dialogue, who does not offer ideas for examination or discussion – that is the Facilitator. The Facilitator remains outside the circle of the group – partly in order to see everyone and partly to set that distance between the group/community and him/herself. It is the Facilitator who creates the conditions under which an inquiry can take place.

> Reasoning must develop in situations and circumstances which are 'natural' environments for reasoning, in the way in which water is the natural environment for swimming. Those situations in which reasoning is called for, rather than say obeying orders, or making arbitrary decisions, or memorising information, would be 'natural' environments in which to find reasoning.... An environment which

actually calls for reasoning in the sense that swimming actually calls for when in deep water, would be one in which other forms of thought or behaviour would not be successful. And this is what the Community of Philosophical Inquiry does – it calls for reasoning.

(McCall, 1991, p. 17)

And it is this that the Facilitator oversees. The role of the Facilitator is not an easy one – either in practice or in theory. He/she is part of the group and at the same time apart from the group. The Facilitator sets the text for the group and notes down their initial questions arising from the text or that have arisen prompted by what has been read. A question is then selected by the Facilitator for the group to discuss following the set structure and using the rules of the practice. The question will be one wherein the Facilitator sees much scope and potential for *philosophical* dialogue. In 'throwing' the question back to its originator, the Facilitator asks for initial thoughts or comments about the question, why it was asked, perhaps, or what is particularly puzzling about it. Thereafter, if any of the group wishes to comment or contribute he/she must raise his/her hand to indicate a desire to speak. The Facilitator will not necessarily select the speaker in the order the hands were raised. Rather, with his/her overview of the dialogue as a whole and his/her knowledge of the participants and the way they generally contribute to an inquiry, he/she will select a speaker in order to juxtapose arguments in order that the dialogue continually moves forwards; he/she endeavours to create some dynamic within the group which will drive the inquiry further and deeper. The Facilitator's loyalty is to the dialogue rather than to the individuals; he/she creates the environment where an argument is generated and maintained at a philosophical level. Certainly, the Facilitator can ask for clarification or examples to illustrate a point made, but, as Facilitator, one must endeavour not to rephrase or lead the individuals – or dialogue – in a direction of his/her own personal interest; there is no place for a personal agenda within the role of Facilitator. Somewhat like Socrates, the Facilitator is akin to a midwife and aims to deliver the community of its ideas or thoughts, and not always necessarily in a comfortable situation. It is an oft times difficult process giving birth to one's ideas when they challenge assumptions or perspectives one may have felt comfortable or satisfied with.

Like childbirth, coming to new ideas or alternative ways of thinking is a process which takes time and will involve periods of difficulty and periods of clarity – women do not have children without contractions, and philosophizing is not also without its twinges. The metaphor of Socrates as midwife is clearly illustrated in the *Theaetetus*; Socrates here indicates that his task is to '... supervise the labour of their minds' (Plato, 1987b, p. 27). The task Socrates takes upon himself is one that probes – no sooner has Theaetetus offered a suggestion than Socrates is trying to make him push further and harder. Support for Theaetetus' ideas is there, Socrates is promoting Theaetetus' thinking; Theaetetus himself says to his 'midwife' that '... it would be disgraceful for anyone faced with the sort of encouragement you are giving, not to try his hardest to express his thoughts' (*ibid.*, p. 29). Similarly, in a Community of Philosophical Inquiry, it might not be 'disgraceful' not to express one's thoughts or ideas, but it would certainly be surprising since the conditions have been so carefully prepared. Burnyeat too sees Socrates as a midwife in the questions he pursues with his interlocutors, '... his questions will direct a painful process of bringing to birth Theaetetus' own conceptions and then testing for soundness' (1987b, p. 6). While Socrates elicits thinking and ideas from his 'subject' in a very directed fashion, the Facilitator in COPI is much less directed and 'hands on' in approach; his/her presence is not felt in such an obvious manner. However, the Facilitator could equally say what Socrates says to Theodorus, '... none of the ideas come from me, but always from whomever is talking with me' (Plato, 1987b, p. 47). Taking the midwife metaphor further, the Facilitator ensures that the group is aware that, while the thinking about and challenging of one's assumptions may not be comfortable, that the pregnancy is encouraged and the birth is welcomed. It is important that the Facilitator 'reads' the inquiry in the sense that he/she can interpret the silences that may occur during the session, for instance, the pause may be empty where no one has anything they wish to contribute at that time which would be of benefit to the dialogue, or if, in fact, the silence is 'pregnant', one about to bear valuable philosophical fruit that will point the inquiry in a new and deeper direction. The COPI is such that *all* participants are fertile and with proper propagation will fall pregnant and yield philosophical fruit.

Just as a midwife is trained in the skill of delivering babies into the world, similarly there is an element of training for those electing to be Facilitators. However, unlike the philosopher kings of the *Republic*, they are not selected and moulded from birth, yet, at the same time, it is a skill to be learned and practised too. If the model of COPI were to be used with citizens' juries, it would be easy enough to offer some training for Facilitators too, and these individuals would be monitored in their practice to ensure non-partisan behaviour, that they were not guiding the jury according to a hidden personal agenda. Likewise, though, the Facilitators would be eligible to be a part of citizens' juries or COPIs as *active* participants in order that their views and ideas may be shared and have the same validity as everyone else's in the wider community. It may be suggested that the role of Facilitator in the COPI is to bring about effective reasoning and thinking within a group and that they (the Facilitators) have responsibility to the ideas and not the individuals concerned. Perhaps, then, the notion of person (as previously described) would be changed somewhat, since our goal in such a society would be to further the entity as a whole, to create and maintain a community, encompassing everyone and 'caring' for them in light of the prevalent, ruling, moral code at that time. This would mean the community would be the end that is respected and valued and the individuals would remain persons as they are being treated as such; but at the same time it could be argued that this is treating them as a means to an end. We may, however, get around this issue by suggesting that ultimately the individuals will benefit from the COPI and so they are being treated as ends in themselves, since the idea is to generate community and a common goal which is positive for all concerned. Bearing in mind it has already been posited that through a practice such as COPI or citizens' juries there may be less need for legislature, then what may be required would be administrators to facilitate the smooth running of our community, to allocate funds, to maintain continuity where and when required, to ensure the egalitarian nature of our community that has been modelled on the practice of COPI. Indeed, as McCall (1991) holds,

> Creating conditions which allow for the emergence of both the dis-
> position to inquire and the skills to reason empowers people in a way
> that simple enfranchisement does not. Enfranchisement alone will not
> ensure democracy. But the possession of inquiry and reasoning skills
> empowers by enabling people – adults and children – to seek for and
> deal with the truth – what is there.
>
>   (McCall, 1991, p. 38)

And it is here that McCall raises a crucial issue – the empowerment of children.

Conclusions

It has been argued in this chapter that in order to be an effective citizen one must not only be active in the sense that one votes at general elections, but one should contribute to the political debate about the running of the society of which one is a part. The debate, or dialogue, is political in nature in the sense that moral codes will influence opinion and such dialogue should be used as a tool for change in order to better society. While the notion of citizens' juries has been applauded as a potentially useful means of gauging public opinion and as a method of collating responses to the ways in which society is currently run or about possible policy decisions, the practice of Community of Philosophical Inquiry would perhaps be a more beneficial structure upon which to build the citizens' juries. This practice utilizes a structure which enables individuals to participate on an equal footing under the guidance of a trained Facilitator. The Facilitator has been likened to Socrates in his role as a midwife in that he/she creates a climate or environment whereby participants are all potentially capable of bearing philosophical ideas and ideas that will evolve within a dialogue to create new and deeper understandings. As a practice, Community of Philosophical Inquiry encourages individuals to challenge their own assumptions and the assumptions of others – it is this, it is being suggested, that should be promoted within citizens' juries. Further, as within the rules of COPI, one does not have to offer one's own personally held view or opinion, then the participants within the citizens' jury would be enabled to concentrate on the dialogue. It has also been claimed here that in promoting this form of inquiring one would work towards moving society to that of community as there would be a common and understood goal or purpose – that of the betterment of the society or community for all its members. The final point raised at the end of the chapter is one which is most pertinent if we want to talk in terms of inclusion and empowerment, of participation and egalitarianism – that is the place and empowerment of children in our society.

8

Children as *Beings*

Following on from the discussion of the practice of Community of Philosophical Inquiry (COPI), this chapter will address how this relates to children and their empowerment within society. It will be claimed that children have been given a voice in a tokenistic sense and that their voice is limited and controlled by the adults within society. As children are socialized in their 'becoming' they undergo, it will be posited, a moulding and shaping that will see them receive full adulthood which will culminate in full person-hood. The idea of child as citizen will be explored and will be considered in terms of rights and responsibilities. The chapter will review the role of the child and how they have been not only kept outside the space of moral issues but also that they are completely outside the political world. The idea that through Community of Philosophical Inquiry children may be encouraged to be more active participants in the sense of being full citizens in their political participation will also be examined.

Child Citizens

We are coming closer to the impetus behind this book; this may be the point when we can truly say what it means, or is, to be a *child*. Clearly, if McCall (1991) discusses the empowerment of children, then she considers them to be lacking in power or authority within our society, she wishes to promote their 'voices' or give them some kind of participatory role. It is true to say that more and more adults are living their lives without children of their own, but this means, as Qvortrup *et al.* indicate that a larger '... part of the electorate which has nothing at stake as far as children are concerned is growing' (1994, p. 18) and are therefore making decisions on their behalf. Indeed, children's lives are almost totally directed and controlled by the adult population with little more than a nod in the direction of the individuals such policy-making concerns. Prout and James (1997) highlight this anomaly when they say that

> Despite our recognition that children are active social beings, it remains true that their lives are almost always determined and/or constrained in large measure by adults and there are few instances of children becoming organized at a 'grass roots' level to represent themselves independently. On the contrary, almost all political, educational, legal and administrative processes have profound effects on children but they have little or no influence over them.
>
> (Prout and James, 1997, p. 29)

This is exactly where children are discriminated against within our society, they are not considered as equal to other groups within society, that is, adult groups, and thus the notion of children as inferior members of society is constructed and repeatedly reinforced. As Qvortrup (1997) states,

> Giving children a voice as a collectivity amounts to representing them on equal terms with other groups in society. Seeing children on equal terms with adults in itself contradicts our 'adultist' imagery, exactly because it cuts across prefigured conceptions of children as subordinates.
>
> (Qvortrup, 1997, p. 87)

If we are to give children a voice socially and politically we must be prepared that we will be challenging the ways in which children are currently viewed by society and we would thus be challenging, in some way, the accepted social order. Children are not treated as equals and as such different things are expected from them than from the adult members of society, however, note that the expectations are set by *adults* within society.

Let us consider what is expected of children with respect to their obligations in society. In the *polis* of Athens the job or role of citizen was undertaken seriously; the *polis* was primarily before individuals. Faulks suggests that in ancient Athens '... from birth, citizens internalised the values of active citizenship, greatly influencing the content and depth of its practice' (2000, p. 16). Implicit within the statement is the fact that one was a citizen *at birth*; similarly, it was the case that the child of a slave was born a slave. This links strongly to the idea posited in Chapter One that personhood is attributed at birth and one can only 'resign' from this status by breaking the rules for personhood within the culture in which one finds oneself. Likewise, Rousseau (1948) suggests that we can break our citizenhood by breaking the contract we hold within our society:

> ... for by a right which nothing can abrogate, every man, when he comes of age, becomes his own master, free to renounce the contract by which he forms part of the community, by leaving the country in which that contract holds good.
>
> (Rousseau, 1948, p. 419)

It is evident from this too that Rousseau believes we have an obligation within society until we renounce it by taking ourselves out of the society within which we have been placed. He earlier stated, in *Emile*, that '... the idea of social relations is gradually developed in the child's mind, before he can really be an active member of human society' (*ibid.*, p. 156), thus illustrating the belief that social structures with their values and obligations are taught and learned from infancy, since Rousseau held that as individuals our value is dependent upon the society or community to which we belong. Jenks (1996) asserts,

> All sociologies, in their variety of forms, relate to the childhood experience through theories of socialization, whether in relation to the institutional contexts of the family, the peer group or the school.

These three sites are regarded as the serious arenas when the child is most systematically exposed to concerted induction procedures. It is here that the child, within the social system, relates as a subordinate to the formalized strategies of constraint, control, inculcation and patterning which will serve to transform his or her status into the tangible and intelligent form of an adult competent being.

(Jenks, 1996, p. 35)

Acceptable Children

This notion of the child becoming into acceptable adulthood – 'competent' adulthood – begins early in life in order that we recognize our role – our future adult role, our future adult role as citizen. This is not a new notion; Lyman Jr. traces this lack of moral ability, this lack of knowing how one should behave back to the early medieval period when children were seen '... as less capable than older people and should be "strengthened" to learn how to be moral' (1995, p. 93). Being moral is an attribute preserved for adulthood, and a citizen is certainly someone of moral worth, but it is important that children are inculcated into the ways of morality, that they learn what will be expected of them as members of society, and this initiation takes place during one's childhood. Shamgar-Handelman (1994) suggests

From the collective perspective, childhood should be described as that period of time in each person's life which society allocates for the process of training to become the kind of member that the society wants him/her to be ... During this period, different agencies of society are expected to ensure that the child will be transformed into an adult in accordance with the adult-image acceptable in that society.

(Shamgar-Handelman, 1994, p. 250)

Children thus learn the acceptable patterns of behaviour and how to regulate these patterns through the adults they encounter who will model what is acceptable, appropriate and adult and will highlight and eradicate behaviours which fail to fit into these categories of acceptableness, appropriateness or adultness.

Rousseau contradicts his own notion that one is a citizen until potentially one breaks the social contract at maturity as he acknowledges that 'To form citizens is not the work of a day ... it is necessary to educate them when they are children' (1973, p. 147). He believes that what we ought to learn as children is what we will need to practise as adults. It appears that the only obligation or duty a child must perform in society is that one must learn – by whatever means – how to conduct oneself in society. Values and cultural norms should be absorbed in order that the prevalent moral code be maintained, it would seem, without question or contradiction. Jenks (1996) echoes this notion,

> In an unsocialized state the child is manifestly profane, it threatens to bring down social worlds and the threat can only be mollified within theory by treating the child through an archetype as a proto-adult. This socialization theory makes sense of the child as a potential and inevitable supplicant at the altar of the corporate rationality implicit within the social system.

> (Jenks, 1996, p. 20)

He goes on to state that 'In an efficient, "caring" society child-rearing and education liberate the individual into compliance' (*ibid.*, p. 43). There is currently a large move within the British education sectors – prompted by governmental policy – that citizenship be taught as part of the school curriculum. Again, this suggests that education or schooling is a preparation for adulthood and the moral codes deemed 'valuable' by the acting adult moral majority – children must learn how to behave in the adult world. It appears that Citizenship Education is masking what may be called moral education, and in moral education, it is to be understood that one is here talking about determining behaviour and dictating what is reasonable and acceptable behaviour. Downie maintains that it is important that children are taught – or even trained – that their desires should be '... directed towards socially permissible or desirable ends. And in general moral education is directed at character-building and the creation of a socially desirable pattern of desires' (1971, p. 65). Downie's view may appear at first glance to be somewhat 'old fashioned', but whether we call it 'character-building' or citizenship, it amounts to the same thing in negative terms – that society wishes to control its future citizens and it does so through education. Lawson (2001) too sees the negative, and somewhat worrying, aspect of training young people in schools – one of the institutions established by the State:

> Rather than relying on the slow process of attitudinal change, or tackling the root causes of social issues such as racism or youth disaffection, the government is imposing their set of values on individuals with the caution that, if those individuals do not accept them, they will not be able to claim their rights of citizenship. Implicit within this is the idea that we should not be concerned about reasons for participation and motivations for actions. Rather than attempting a wholesale shift in attitude, it is appearances that matter.
>
> (Lawson, 2001, p. 168)

This is something akin to the issue raised earlier that actions, not intentions, are what count toward citizen status in the example that one may be performing citizenly duties or acts by virtue of one's occupation.

Before even formal schooling plays its part in the formation of the child as future participant in society, the family has a key role. It is within the family that we first learn how the social system works. The child is *part* of the system, yet he/she must learn his/her place and what is expected of him/her as a child and, in the future, as an adult. This is more like the training one gives a pet dog – with rewards and punishments we train it to sit, stay, roll over, give a paw or not sit on the furniture – it soon learns its place within the social hierarchy of the household. Similarly, so does the child – and in much the same way. Kennedy highlights this when he suggests that 'She is born into and grows up in a world physically scaled to adults, and scheduled, planned, ordered and controlled by them' (2006, p. 15). James *et al.* (1998) similarly raise this issue, but recognize even more of a power relationship that holds children in the position of the less powerful when they say,

The individual child, it would appear, emerges via the disciplined, spatial implementation of the timetable which instils a regularity and rhythm in all the activities and tasks of children, including control of the material body through the performance of duty and style of life. So, for example, just as soldiers are drilled persistently even beyond basic training, so children are required to eat, sleep, wash and excrete at specific and regular times.

(James *et al.*, 1998, p. 55)

Controlling Children

The amount of control children have over their own lives is extremely limited, not only in the example of children being like soldiers, but in other spheres of their social lives. Limitations are frequently placed on children and they must learn these limitations in order that they know their place in the hierarchy that is our society. In Britain there is a nine o'clock 'watershed' where pro- grammes with a particular content – a content deemed too 'adult', perhaps because of sex, violence or the use of 'strong' language – are postponed until after the watershed when it is assumed children will be either in bed or parents will not have such programmes on the television because they are aware of the potential content at this time of night. Similarly, cinemas rate films with a particular cer- tificate which is allocated according to age; for example there are films where one must be over 12, 15 or 18 in order to gain admission to the cinema to watch the film. There is one category which is interesting, that of Parental Guidance where there seems to be some ambiguity in making the decision that children should not be exposed to whatever form of adult behaviour is depicted on the screen and the censors allow that parents may decide if the material is appropriate for their child. Other such limitations on children are often limits on their physical freedom, for instance, curfews imposed by parents or the police or the opportunity for females under 16 to take the contraceptive pill. James *et al.* highlight further how children's lives are dictated by the adults in the society around them:

...children's access to and participation in a diversity of social arenas becomes proscribed: children's time is inextricably linked with the social space of childhood. ... Primarily, this is achieved through the setting of various age limits to – to list just a few – school attendance, access to work, voting rights, TV and film viewing, leisure activities, geographical mobility, financial transactions, sexual intimacy, property ownership, independent decision-making, criminal blame and personal responsibility.

(*ibid.*, p. 75)

Children want to be 'adult', they mimic the behaviour they see around them and when they do this they sometimes happen upon behaviour which is deemed 'too adult' and are then pushed back into their place, a place of passivity where they are subject, but where they will learn how best to get what they want – access to the adult world. Brennan and Noggle hold that this imitation of those forming a child's social circle is an innate desire, which, one may suggest, is capitalized upon by the ruling adult members of society: 'These role-models arouse the child's innate desire to imitate, causing the child to further internalize the standards of the group by imitating those who conform to them' (1998, p. 216).

Adults possess an inordinate amount of power and control over children and their desire to be 'grown-up', to be adult. Adults determine not only what is acceptable behaviour for an individual, but this is further extended by determining how children will – in future – participate in society, they are shaping *future* citizens. Like personhood, citizenhood is perceived to be a valuable and desirable thing to possess, yet it is becoming ever more evident that for children, while they are being trained in the ways of being citizens, they are not – as children – permitted to practise their citizening skills. Archard calls the adult in control of a child the 'caretaker' – a generous term when one considers that he states the role of caretaker as one who '... chooses for the child in the person of the adult which the child is not yet but will eventually be' (1993, p. 53). James *et al.* (1998) recognize the dangers that are inherent in handing over power and decision-making to a 'caretaker', although one should bear in mind that children have not handed over power or authority to adult caretakers; they never had the power to hand over in the first place and these adults act on what they remember as their experience of having been a child. They claim that

> Given the strategic advantages that adults have in exercising power over children in an adult-centred world, it is always possible, indeed likely, that the processes by which children's preferences enter decision-making will themselves shape the effect they have. In some cases this translation is obvious: children are either not taken into account at all or views are given on their behalf by adults who claim the right to know what is in children's interests. Sometimes this is because it is assumed that, having once been children, all adults know what it is like to be a child. This is of course highly questionable.
>
> (James *et al.*, 1998, p. 144)

Rousseau (1973) firmly holds that children should be taught in a manner that will encourage them, in the future, to see the State, society, in a familial way. They should learn that they have a responsibility or duty to the State and the will of the majority – he is keen to stress the obedience that one should demonstrate.

> If there are laws for the age of maturity, there ought to be laws for infancy, teaching obedience to others: and as the reason of each man is not left to be the sole arbiter of his duties, government ought the less indiscriminately to abandon to the intelligence and prejudices of fathers the education of their children, as that education is of still greater importance to the State than to the fathers: for, according to the course of nature, the death of a father often deprives him of the fruits of education; but his country sooner or later perceives its effects. Families dissolve, but the State remains.
>
> (Rousseau, 1973, p. 148)

The family is perhaps the first model we encounter of a political society and then we move on to school. There are power and authority structures in place in both of these institutions and the child quickly learns how to work within and around them since the child is never one to be in the seat of power or authority in either of these contexts. McGowan Tress (1998) tells us that

In the *polis*, the child's formation occurs through the effect of the lawgiver's regulations and through *polis* schools. The *polis* thus has a major role in the child's development, namely, the cultivation of the human capacity for participation in the city's cultural and political life.

(McGowan Tress, 1998, p. 32)

The *polis'* method of 'cultivating' this future participation was through family and school.

McGowan Tress, in discussing Aristotle's view of children, suggests that

Education should be directed to the needs connected with one's role in adult life, especially the needs of statesmen and citizens. But in the best-governed state, all citizens will share, in turn, in ruling and being ruled. Thus a single plan of education, shared by all citizens' children as potential rulers is appropriate.

(*ibid.*, p. 33)

While he suggests that Aristotle believed very young children, those under five, should be preoccupied with play rather than study or intensive exercise, he does say that the play of the infant should not be undirected, it should be geared towards promoting some kind of virtuous life – which would, one may suggest, involve undertaking citizen duties. Unlike the philosophers chosen at birth within Plato's *Republic* to rule in their maturity, here McGowan Tress is suggesting that Aristotle believed everyone had the potential to be ruler. In the sense that in participating within the structure of electing a government to represent one's moral code publicly or in being a part of a citizens' jury to influence policy-making, then perhaps one *is* a ruler in some sense of the word. Building upon the point that children should be trained for the role they will later undertake, one can see that this role-playing begins early on in one's life, in the family, school and other social groups. Emmet explains how this may be the case: 'In a role one sees oneself in a situation in relation to others who also have their parts in the situation' (1966, p. 140). She goes on to state that

Sometimes changes in circumstances, and sometimes new ways in which some dominant individual plays a role, will establish a new pattern, and make it necessary to form a new concept of a new role type, or a different content to the old one.

(ibid., p. 148)

This is perhaps currently the case with the advent of 'tweenagers'.

The Child Role

Teenagers were conceptualized in the 1950s as a half-way house between childhood and adulthood; now we find tweenagers falling between childhood and teenagehood. This is the fastest growing consumer group in Britain and tweenagers are increasingly having more of an influence on society as a result. Yet, the roles of tweenager and teenager are still within the scope and sphere of childhood, so are then still bound by the rules and roles of being children. Emmet suggests that

What people think they ought to do depends largely on how they see their roles, and (most importantly) the conflicts between their roles. It may be a bridge notion between myself as an individual, with my proper name and my personal responsibility, and my 'station and its duties' in the institutional world of the society in which I have to live.

(ibid., p. 15)

The difference here is that Emmet gives us the power to ascribe ourselves roles, or at least describe how we are to perform that role. The point about the role of *child* is that, like that of *person*, it is *given*, as is the expected behaviour and values that go along with it. Very quickly the child learns his or her role through the ways in which people react and respond to him or her, which in turn begins to develop the idea of where one 'fits in' and so begins to shape the self of the child, but the self can only be shaped in relation to one's interactions with others. Even if one does not interact with others, this non-interaction is still a shaping device and will ultimately bear on how one places oneself in the social hierarchy and thus on one's role. Elkin and Handel (1978) make a similar point when they claim that

> ... by being cared for, by evoking response and being responded to, the infant obtains its first sense of self, first sense of another person, first experience of a social relationship. In this relationship the infant develops its first expectations and thus its first sense of social order.
>
> (Elkin and Handel, 1978, p. 43)

Once the child has begun to assimilate this sense of self as he/she more and more adopts the 'appropriate' role, he/she will then begin to understand what is expected in terms of performance and behaviour and what is not acceptable within the society into which it has been born. So perhaps, then, there are only two duties or obligations that a child is expected to undertake. First, he/she must be 'available', make an effort and be receptive to the training which prepares one for adulthood and citizenship within society, and secondly, that one adopts the role 'child' and conducts oneself in the expected and appropriate manner, especially in relation to others. As Emmet (1966) suggests,

> The notion of *role* ... provides a link between factual descriptions of social situations and moral pronouncements about what ought to be done in them. It has, so to speak, a foot in both camps, that of fact and of value; it refers to a relationship with a factual basis, and it has a norm of behaviour built into it which is being explicitly or tacitly accepted if the role is cited as a reason.
>
> (Emmet, 1966, p. 41)

A relevant example may be when a child is upset with another child and hits out. A nearby adult might suggest that he/she does not know any better, he/she 'is only a child'. This behaviour, while expected as part of being a child, is excused for the same reason. However, under the child's obligation to learn how one behaves in one's adult role in society, one will come to learn that hitting out is not acceptable behaviour and therefore not within the role of adult or in being a *person*. It was seen earlier that in return for fulfilling one's obligations or duties one received certain privileges in the form of rights.

Privileges in some sense are perhaps contrary to the notion of rights. It may be posited that rights are things we are entitled to by virtue of our existence, yet if we are given personhood and citizenhood at birth, we automatically inherit the duties discussed before. However, merely because one has been born into a society where certain things are expected, an entitlement to rights does not automatically follow. It is therefore preferable to talk of rights in terms of privileges – made and attributed by humans, much like citizenhood and personhood, rather than being natural in origin – they would not, and could not, exist without people. Bellamy, who was in 1996 the Executive Director of Unicef, advocates a world of rights for children which allows that they have more of a participatory role within society. She claims that what is needed is

> . . . a new vision of the child – not as a mini-adult or as a minor, but rather as a developing human being, endowed with all rights from the beginning, and growing to contribute to his or her society. The convention [on the Rights of the Child] considers the child a person, and children's essential needs as rights which the adult world – individuals, families, communities and governments – are obligated to respect and fulfil.
>
> (Bellamy, 1996, p. 10)

It is all very well and commendable that children should be perceived of as persons, for we have seen that in order to maintain one's personhood one must treat others as persons; this is where the Convention falls down. While the Convention claims that children are persons, *nowhere* does it say exactly how the Convention – and those upholding the Convention – define the notion of *person*, although it does imply that in being a person one has rights, and so, children must be enabled to avail themselves of these rights.

The Child with Rights

Cunningham (1995) tells us

> In thinking of the late nineteenth and early twentieth centuries the rights of children were entirely consonant with an increased role for the state in the lives of children. For it was the state alone which could enforce those rights.
>
> (Cunningham, 1995, p. 161)

Throughout the twentieth century and into this new century, the movement towards increased rights for children has gathered impetus. This is echoed somewhat by Verhellen when he suggests that 'New understandings of childhood and changing perceptions of children have led to children's right to enjoy their rights in the here and now being widely advocated' (2000, p. 34). It is perhaps worth noting that the rights afforded children are certainly being legitimized by the State in its legislation, however, the interesting issue is that it is the adult population that is determining what rights should be in place. In fact, this very issue is discussed by Boyden (1997) when she considers how little a role – none in fact – children had in forming the Convention on the Rights of the Child, and equally they have had no input on how best to implement the decisions taken for them and about them since the Convention's inception. She says all this

> In spite of the fact that the treaty not only recognizes the vulner-abilities of children but also their capacities, endorsing in articles 12 to 15 the notion that children capable of forming their own views have a right to participate in decisions and all matters affecting them.
>
> (Boyden, 1997, p. 222)

So while advocating children's rights, the Convention manages to fall foul of its own intentions. However, at least in considering the issue one may argue that a new perspective is being put on the notion of childhood and it is this reconstruction that is of value. Matthews points out, 'As we saw during the civil rights movement of the 1960s, recognising the moral rights of a certain group of people often encourages us to change our moral attitudes toward them as well' (1994, p. 69).

This perhaps supports the notion discussed in a previous chapter that we maintain our individual personhood by treating others well, as persons; this is an obligation of personhood. While the point of citizenship is to work for the betterment of society as a whole rather than concentrating one's efforts on specific individuals or groups within society, there is the danger that minority groups – and children fall into this category – may have their behaviour and living conditions dictated by a more powerful group such as adult society, which in turn would lead to a suppression of rights for the minority group. It is wise to be careful in considering the ways and practices that are used to afford children protection; Qvortrup (1997) highlights the importance of just why some forms of protection may be negative:

> While it is of course in many ways reasonable to protect children, it must be added that protection is mostly accompanied by exclusion in one way or another; protection may be suggested even when it is not strictly necessary for the sake of children, but rather works to protect adults or the adult social orders against disturbances from the presence of children. This is exactly the point at which protection threatens to slide into unwarranted dominance.
>
> (Qvortrup, 1997, p. 86)

The notion of citizenship and how active one is, or is allowed to be, is an issue of power and in the context of children and adults, children certainly have the less powerful stance and are thus limited in the contributions they can make because of this powerful 'dominance' adults have over them. deWinter also adopts this line: '... citizenship proves to work as a social dividing line; between active and inactive people, between the powerful and the powerless and, significant in this context, between adults and the young' (1997, p. 30). So, while adult society is issuing decrees about children's rights and entitlements, adults are still very much in control, driving the issues and agendas of what children's entitlement should be and in what ways they can participate. Children are given rights, but there seems little purpose in providing rights if children cannot avail themselves of the rights involved, or, in point of fact, *if* they want these rights in the first place since they have been instituted by the adult majority group.

Mill (1985) states,

> Over himself, over his own body and mind the individual is sovereign. It is, perhaps, hardly necessary to say that this doctrine is meant to apply only to human beings in the maturity of their faculties. We are not speaking of children or young persons below the age which the law may fix as that of manhood or womanhood. Those who are still in a state to require being taken care of by others must be protected against their own actions as well as against external injury.
>
> (Mill, 1985, p. 69)

Mill, here, is not taking account of the fact first that the younger members of our society may in actual fact be very capable of taking care of themselves and others; think of, for instance, children caring on a daily basis for parents with disabilities. Secondly, he fails to acknowledge that the actions of the younger individual are not necessarily irresponsible or working against the betterment of the society or community. One need hardly mention that there are countless 'adult' members of society that cannot fend for themselves for a variety of reasons, for example, disability, prejudice, illness, unemployment, and so on. In fact, perhaps the only factor that precludes children from Mill's model of society is that they do not earn a wage with which to pay their way or provide for themselves – the Citizens' Income may take care of this. It could be argued, however, that in opting to have children one is bound to provide and care for them until legally they are able to gain employment and, therefore, become fully self-sufficient. This legal aspect is an interesting one since pre-eighteenth century there was little notion that children should not go out to work to 'earn their keep'; so it is the policy makers in our society that set the parameters for children's working hours and conditions in an endeavour to preserve childhood – whatever that may be. King, in discussing

Hobbes' view of children, suggests that '... there is nothing special about the rights exercised over children or the feeble, they are just easier to subdue than others in the state of nature' (1998, p. 69). And so, this is the background which has led to the United Nations (UN) debating the rights of the child and establishing a convention which certain countries have agreed to set as their marker for the treatment of children and the rights they are entitled to claim.

Child Power

Within Article 1 it is clearly stated that 'For the purpose of the present Convention a child means every human being below the age of 18 years unless, under the law applicable to the child, majority is attained earlier' (Newell, 1991, p. 2). This is possibly the first clear statement of what a child *is*, albeit one that conforms to a chronological presence on the planet. Even so, this article shies away from a full commitment which would establish 18 as *the* age when one ceases to be a child; the clause '... unless, under the law applicable to the child, majority is attained earlier' gives individual countries the wherewithal to deny the rights established by the Convention. This also excludes any country setting a minimum age limit for adulthood and the loss of children's rights above the age of 18 if they are to be recognized by the UN and the Convention. Newell highlights a further interesting and potentially difficult issue,

> The wording of the Convention leaves open the starting point for childhood – is it birth, conception or somewhere in between? The deliberate intention was to avoid entangling the Convention in debates concerning abortion, embryo research and other highly charged issues which might well have threatened its adoption in many countries.
>
> (*ibid.*, p. 2)

Perhaps one might argue that at the point of conception one is a child, but at that point one is not a *person* under the definition we previously employed, that in order to be a person one has to be able to treat others as persons, and since, in the womb, the child is incapable of treating others (its mother) as persons it cannot be perceived as such. One may also wish to say that the child in the womb is treating its mother as a means and not as an end in herself, which would further negate the idea of the foetus being a person. However, those outside the womb must treat the child *as* a person in order to retain their personhoods. This raises the thorny issue of abortion which will not be discussed here, but one should bear in mind that there may be implications for the mother and doctor in terms of *their* personhoods if they undertake the killing of what some consider to be human life.

So, while the age of 18 has been suggested as the time when one is no longer a child (although still a 'teenager'), we are no clearer about when one becomes a child, how long one is a child for, or – and more importantly – what a child actually *is*. We have, however, formulated some rights which this ambiguous group are able to access.

The Rt. Hon. Lord Justice Sedley, in response to the subject of rights, holds that 'Fundamental rights are expressed in general terms. How they are interpreted will change as society changes' (2000, p. 10). This comment is interesting on two counts. First there is the assumption that rights are things we are entitled to possess by virtue of having been born and secondly, that rights may be static, but how they are implemented or accessed may change over time. It may be claimed that rights cannot be fundamental in that it is society, and therefore, human beings, that constitute them. What is particularly interesting about the Convention's articles, is that there are no rights there listed that are not also afforded to adults. This is possibly where the confusion lies with this relatively new concept of *child*; that we are coming full circle again and are giving children the opportunity to be adults, or to perform the adult role. Thus, in the vast majority of respects we still want these individuals to be children and the method we have for preserving this state is power. As Wringe states, 'The connection between rights and power or powers would seem particularly relevant to any discussion of children's rights' (1981, p. 23). And it is this 'adult' power that acts most effectively by not promoting the younger members of our society within the decision-making process, they are given a voice when adults see fit. Interestingly, this appears to be the main thrust of the Convention that has been taken up most strongly within our society and more specifically in the present Government's push for Citizenship Education. Aristotle (1955) would hold that there is no place for politics in the life of children and no place for children in the life of politics:

> Every man is a good judge of what he understands: in special subjects the specialist, over the whole field of knowledge the man of general culture. This is the reason why political science is not a proper study for the young. The young man is not versed in the practical business of life from which politics draws its premises and its data.
>
> (Aristotle, 1955, p. 28)

Aristotle can relax, for while Citizenship Education is becoming ever more present in schools, little of its content has to do with the politics of the wider society and even where it does stray into this realm, children are firmly kept in their place until old enough to participate on the political stage.

Newell (1991) would support the claim that children are kept at a distance to the political world that acts on their behalf and suggests that

> Children lack an effective voice in political systems; even, generally, in the services and institutions designed exclusively 'for' them. They face unique discrimination on grounds of their age and status, and may face the double jeopardy of additional discrimination on grounds such as disability, race, culture, gender, class and poverty.
>
> (Newell, 1991, p. xi)

There is much to contend with here, yet, in allowing a space or opportunity for views to be taken account of, the status of children may be improved upon. In being receptive to the views of this group – not even a minority group in the sense of the numbers belonging to it – true representation can be provided. The sticking point is not so much that children be enabled to express their views, it is more that those with power are determining whether or

not the views are considered and 'reasonable'. Newell suggests that
Article 12 '... is the cornerstone of the Convention's insistence that
children must not be treated as silent objects of concern, but as
people with their own views and feelings which must be taken
seriously' (*ibid.*, p. 44). It may be suggested that what this article
means is that children should be treated as *persons*. Article 12 states
that children have the right to develop their own views, ideas and
opinions freely without external interference of this freedom – yet,
there are still restrictions in the sense that maturity of reasoning,
age, ability to articulate are all heavily cited, yet these are not
factors (other than age) that are confined to children. Archard
maintains that the denial of rights and entitlements is not solely
based on age, but that 'It is done on the basis of an alleged cor-
relation between age and some relevant competence ... being
young, they are presumed to lack some capacities necessary for the
possession of rights' (1993, p. 58). Children's powers of reasoning,
argumentation and their ability to listen and take on board alternative ideas are given little emphasis which is perhaps why the
adult/child divide persists; it suits the adult power holders that
children's views can be expressed, and possibly be taken account of,
but that they are much less able to reason than the adults – not
true! Archard highlights exactly why children are excluded from
the adult world of reason and understanding, he says that

> For us childhood is a stage or state of incompetence relative to
> adulthood. The ideal adult is equipped with certain cognitive capa-
> cities, rational, physically independent, autonomous, has a sense of
> identity and is conscious of its beliefs and desires, and thus able to
> make informed free choices for which it can be held personally
> responsible ... It is precisely because the child lacks these adult dis-
> positions that it may not participate in this adult world.
>
> (*ibid.*, p. 30)

In many ways children are what women once were – and to a
certain extent still are – within the power structures of society, as
Faulks (2000) states,

Women have often appeared to be faced with the choice of whether to argue for incorporation into an inherently masculine conception of citizenship, an incorporation that can only be achieved by denying their differences from men, or whether to assert a politics of difference, which jettisons ideas of universal citizenship and argues instead for special rights and responsibilities. However, there is no reason to suppose that equality and difference are inherently in opposition.

(Faulks, 2000, p. 99)

The only difference between this picture of women and the situation in which children find themselves – and it is quite a major point – is that women, by virtue of being seen to be adults, have still more power than children to create a role or agenda for themselves. As Archard indicates, 'For Locke it is adult human beings who make the contract, and consequently enjoy the protection of their rights under civil government. Children are neither parties to the contract nor right-holding citizens of the government thereby agreed to' (1998, p. 92).

Future Citizens

Certainly it is adult human beings that set the agenda or contract, yet children are obliged, as was suggested earlier, to abide by the contract although they are still not citizens in the sense that at present the voice of children is somewhat tokenistic with inroads only being made in May 2002 with the United Nations Special Session on Children, a consultation with children representatives from around the world. It remains to be seen what influence these and subsequent children's views have had on the policy-makers from the adult community also attending this and similar summits. A common misconception put forward by King, in taking account of Hobbes, is that '... it is precisely because children cannot see the consequences of their actions that they cannot enter into a covenant' (1998, p. 77). However, the same could be said for many older members of society. Further, while not formally accepting a covenant – since their voices and actions are somewhat determined by external forces – children do comply with the covenant or contract as part of their obligations in order that they gain membership to society, maintain their personhood, strive towards citizenhood and 'grow' into adulthood. Archard indicates Locke's agreement with this perception of children '... as the recipients of an ideal upbringing, citizens in the making, fledgling but imperfect reasoners, and blank sheets filled by experience' (1998, p. 85). Again it seems that since children are not considered suitably adept as reasoners, they cannot be citizens in their own right. Faulks (2000) clearly states that

> Active citizenship begins with the individual, since it is through individual actions that the structural conditions of citizenship are reproduced and improved. Political reform must look to improve the opportunities for citizens to exercise their rights and responsibilities by promoting an ethic of participation.
>
> (Faulks, 2000, p. 108)

This is as true for our younger members of society as for our more established ones – we must promote an ethos whereby individuals see and understand the need for cooperation and interdependence for the creation of a community.

Citizenship Education is one of the latest buzz words in schools, colleges, universities, newspapers and politics at this point in time. Perhaps there is some realization that everyone acting as an individual to further his/her own gains works against the advancement of society as a whole. There are, though, some aspects of this movement which may cause concern. Lawson suggests that it appears that classes in citizenship '... are promoting a form of citizenship education that teaches people what they need to know to cope with life and society as it is, rather than providing opportunities for discussing and challenging issues and questioning the status quo' (2001, p. 176).

Lessons on drugs and sex are incorporated within citizenship classes which appear to be lessons on morality more than, as Lawson suggested, places where pupils can raise issues of concern in order to debate and discuss them, that is, issues that are of concern to them *now*, not when they are older individuals with all the power that entails. Somehow the citizenship classes imply some kind of control, where the accepted moral code is held to be the way forward and the route into adult life and full citizenship. Archard indicates the reasoning behind the interest in children in terms of their schooling and citizenship education: 'The State may claim a legitimate interest in the welfare of children both as *current* human beings to be cared for and as *future* citizens who must now be trained for their eventual roles in society' (1993, p. 112).

One wonders if it is possible to fail these classes in citizenship and what one would have to do in order to fail. Even the notion of the classes, set aside, compartmentalized times for certain issues to be raised is peculiar. Issues affecting our personhood and/or citizenhood permeate all areas of our lives and within school (and outside) there should be opportunities to discuss and explore these matters. Indeed, Lawson (2001) makes the pertinent point that

> Telling pupils what to think as opposed to how to think has certain implications. The outcome may be positive for society in the short term but this approach leaves no room for real debate and does not allow for individuals to explore issues for themselves and reach their own conclusions.
>
> (Lawson, 2001, p. 171)

We cannot consider moral issues by simply doing as we are told by the power or authority in charge – this is the case both in schools and the wider world, both for school pupils and those outwith formal education. Lawson suggests that 'A connection is thus established between formal education and adult behaviour, with the underlying supposition that a predilection for action in later life will be gained through participating in community activities at school' (*ibid.*, p. 170). After all, it is this promotion of community spirit which will, it is hoped, work within a society in order to create and maintain an active community with an effective – and active – citizenry, fulfilling obligations and maintaining the provision for the rights received under the reciprocal relationship formally established by society – or rather, the individuals working together that constitute that society. We should take care not to confuse the idea of 'community spirit' with the controlling of behaviour and moral codes. Kennedy warns us of the potential uses of the school community, that 'The school as embryonic community is in fact a laboratory for relations of power – a site necessary to any collective interested in social reconstruction' (2006, p. 163). The notion of community should be concerned with the sharing of ideas and opinions in order to better society as a whole. 'Better' needing to be defined through dialogue, discussion and debate as the members of a society may not – indeed, probably will not – all agree on how they may define the 'betterment' of society.

Plato (1987a) is particularly clear about what society should do in order that effective citizens are produced:

> By maintaining a sound system of education and upbringing you produce citizens of good character; and citizens of sound character, with the advantage of a good education, produce in turn children better than themselves and better able to produce still better children in their turn, as can be seen with animals.
>
> (Plato, 1987a, p. 132)

For Plato it was important that order and respect for order be learned at an early age; even the games of children should teach these orderly habits and built into these games would be the opportunity for correcting or altering 'flaws' that may exist in a society, so that they may be eradicated over time as the youngsters progress to being fully active citizens. Plato is even more prescriptive regarding the organization of the young and how they should learn for the betterment of society, although in referring to ten year olds as citizens, it could be argued that in this instance citizen should be read to mean 'resident'.

> They [the Rulers] would begin by sending away into the country all citizens over the age of ten; having thus removed the children from the influence of their parents' present way of life, they would bring them up in their own methods and rules, ... This is the best and quickest way to establish our society and constitution, and for it to

prosper and bring its benefits to any people among which it is established.

(*ibid.*, p. 293)

The intention is that the children would not have free rein until they had learned the societal structures and until they had been educated for their future role in life. This, it could be argued, is how Citizenship Education is manifesting itself today in some ways. However, Plato was ahead of today's educators or policy makers to some extent – he held firmly that children be encouraged to philosophize which is more closely related to the United Nations Convention on the Rights of the Child and its assertions that children should have their views heard and acted upon. While the Convention does not overtly advocate children philosophizing, this seems a natural way to accommodate hearing children's views and enabling them to have a voice by giving them the necessary tools to listen, discuss, debate and change their views and the views of others. In fact, since November 2006, United Nations Educational Scientific and Cultural Organization (UNESCO) has been con-sulting those working in the field of Philosophy with Children to ascertain exactly what may be gained from encouraging children to philosophize. Matthews (1998), in considering Socrates and Socrates' view of children suggests that

> Socratic questioning, we could almost say, began as philosophy for children. ... Certainly it included philosophy for children from the first. Socrates himself seems to have found it entirely appropriate to engage children in philosophical discussion; moreover, he clearly respected children as philosophical discussion partners.

(Matthews, 1998, p. 12)

Philosophical Children

Lipman talks of Callicles in the *Gorgias*, insinuating that '... philosophy is for children only: grown-ups had better get on with the serious business of life' (1988, p. 3). This is a move away from the idea that children are non or pre-rational beings; Callicles is certainly affording children some commendation that is often not readily attributed, however, he does abstract the child from the 'serious business of life'. All members of society participate to a greater or lesser degree in society and life in general, and younger members of society have much to contribute as they form a large proportion of the physical world of life. Children, it is argued, are as capable and competent of commenting and reflecting upon the 'serious business of life' which ultimately affects their existence and functioning. Perhaps it is not children, as Piaget suggested, that search for finite answers to all questions, but that searching *without* finding a finite answer or coming to some conclusion or consensus is not acceptable to *adults* living in the hustle and bustle of the oftentimes non-reflective 'serious business of life'. Kennedy high-lights the mistaken view commonly held by 'adultist' society that reflects the notion that children are ignorant in the 'serious business of life'; '... one of the major characteristics of adultism is the ignorant attribution of ignorance to children' (2006, p. 162).

Philosophizing in Community of Philosophical Inquiry is per-haps the best method we have for children to participate as citizens within society, even by forming citizens' juries perhaps entirely made up of children and following the COPI model, as discussed previously.

McCall (1991) asserts that

Unlike conceptual inquiry in theoretical physics, very little experience of the world is needed in order to engage in for example metaphysical inquiry. Very little empirical knowledge is required to inquire about the nature of reality, or truth, or justice or beauty. These are basic issues and anyone, no matter how little knowledge they may have can think about them, can reason about them, and can engage in philo-sophical inquiry on these issues.

(McCall, 1991, p. 19)

Very often Communities of Philosophical Inquiry involving eight- or nine-year-old participants will raise the same questions, issues and arguments as a community of participants in their forties, fifties or sixties. The vocabulary, or the availability of extensive examples upon which to draw, are the only differences between these age groups, although, when asked for an example, younger community members are able to provide a very adequate one from their realm of experiences. Further, having a broad ranging vocabulary does not preclude one from finding it difficult to say what one wants to say or say what one means. As McCall correctly highlights,

> Our notion of childhood has many roots, but a recurrent feature in the literature of childhood involves a notion of children as non-rational or pre-rational beings. This feature traditionally relies on two strong lines of support. One line of support stems from developmental cognitive psychology, particularly stage maturation theories, which claim that the cognitive *capacity* for rationality is not present until a person has matured to a certain age (usually around 11 years old). Hence young children could neither think abstractly (i.e. using abstract concepts) nor could they think logically. The other line of support, often found in philosophical accounts, is a definition of rationality which relies on criteria drawn from formal logic. (The latter kinds of definition of rationality, if broadly applied would also exclude many adults from the category of 'rational beings'.)
>
> (*ibid.*, p. 3)

McCall's final point regarding adults is one that is often overlooked, or rather ignored, in the argument that children are not adept reasoners. Matthews discusses a philosophizing session he had with a group of children; they had been discussing a story which centred around the notion of bravery. From the resulting dialogue the children offered criteria of six points that may indicate one's bravery; Matthews claims that '... even though the six points are neither necessary nor sufficient for bravery, they offer a better analysis of bravery than anything one can find in Plato' (1984, p. 23). Matthews has gone on to criticize developmentalists for their influence in the way children are perceived which links strongly with how children are perceived in terms of their reasoning abilities; he says that 'The *idea* of developmental psychology has had a greater influence on the way adults think about children than have any specific theories as to how children develop' (*ibid.*, p. 31). The whole notion of stage maturation theory has disallowed pre-adolescents from being acknowledged as having reasoning powers. On the contrary, from an early age humans are able and competent reasoners and it is through one's usage of these skills that one becomes more able to reason, reflect and analyse. Law discusses what he considers to be good moral education, 'Rather than encouraging them [children] to defer to authority, we should confront young people with their responsibility to think for themselves about right and wrong' (2006, p. 2). This promotion of children thinking for themselves should not be confined to moral or ethical matters, reasoning skills should be practised as widely as possible. Mill acknowledges that 'The mental and the moral, like the muscular, powers are improved only by being used' (1985, p. 122). And this is vital in considering how children are perceived and in what ways they are permitted to be part of society.

Anyone, of whatever age, will develop their reasoning skills with practise – arguments and reasoning will become more complex and 'mature' with practise, not necessarily as a result of the reasoner being older. Certainly the majority of younger individuals have less experience of living in the world than the majority of older individuals, however, it is not necessarily the case that more practical worldly experience will make one a clear and more effective reasoner; in fact, one's thinking may be obscured because one is entrenched and comfortable in the assumptions upon which one's life has become founded. These young people are open to possibilities and should be encouraged to challenge and question the world around them if they are to be effective citizens working to promote community. In 1988 McCall undertook a series of experimental philosophizing sessions with six year olds. Her aim was to find out whether young children could '. . . generate abstract concepts themselves and reason about them, without prior teaching from an adult' (1991, p. 3). The results were illuminating. Not only were the children displaying sophisticated levels of reasoning in their arguments, they had not – prior to these sessions – ever had any input in the form of logical reasoning tasks or any other exercises which would have taught the skills necessary to perform at such an 'advanced' level. Certainly it had been acknowledged previously by the likes of Piaget and other stage maturation theorists, that older children may have the capacity – but not necessarily the ability – to reason in such a manner. The structure used by McCall of the COPI facilitates this type of reasoning in the participants – whatever their age. Indeed, McCall points out that

> ...seeing the children agreeing and disagreeing with each other, adding to the ideas of others, even explaining to other children what they might have been thinking of – all of these behaviours stand as counter-evidence to the assertions of some cognitive psychologists that children are egocentric. Both in the sense of only being willing to consider their own point of view (a characteristic which they would share with adults), and in the sense of being unable to perceive another point of view.
>
> (*ibid.*, p. 26)

Children are, like their older counterparts, empowered by participating in a COPI. While they may not, at present, be in the position to directly influence policy making, they will – through COPI – develop the necessary skills to inquire, think, reason and participate effectively as citizens in the wider community. Individually children can learn how to listen to alternative viewpoints, how to posit alternative viewpoints – even alternatives to what they currently hold – how to build upon previous arguments and develop them whereby they can demonstrate their application in the wider world. Not only will these areas be developed, participants will grow in their social interactions; they will become more aware of how different individuals can be, but at the same time, learn how to work with these different individuals for a common cause. Warnock advocates philosophy, or a philosophical approach, being included within the school curriculum, or rather more as a way of life within the school in an endeavour to prepare children to face the challenges they will encounter throughout their lives. While Warnock suggests this inclusion of philosophy into school life at the upper end of the secondary school, I would advocate that this approach is equally useful at a much earlier point in children's schooling and should be included as soon as possible on entry into school. Warnock (1992) states

> ... the less narrowly a pupil's critical faculties are confined within the bounds of a single set of concepts or procedures, the more easily he will be able to adapt to life after school, whether at work or in higher education, and the more free his imagination will become.
>
> (Warnock, 1992, p. 140)

Warnock, too, however, falls into the trap of seeing children in terms of what they will become and fails to see that the skills acquired during such times when children are encouraged and aided in their reasoning will be of benefit to them in the here and now and not simply when they become adults.

Personalities often diminish within a COPI and a loyalty to the dialogue emerges – it is the discussion and inquiry that become important, but how it could affect people at a group or individual level is often countenanced. Further, within the inquiry, topics arise for consideration that are often not felt suitable or accessible for children; in COPI they are free to discuss subjects usually held onto by the 'adult world' so that they, children, are not 'distressed' by the ideas emerging. There is evidence, through my own facilitation, of Community of Philosophical Inquiry with primary and early secondary school aged participants discussing topics such as death, love, marriage, the existence (or not) of God, terrorism, bigotry, prejudice, truth and justice. Similarly, in adult groups, these subjects have also emerged and often the self-same issues come out in the inquiries, but the children are less inclined to try to stick to a line of reasoning in order to persuade than some adults. They (the children) seem to be more willing to engage fully without the distraction of what they 'know' about how the world external to the COPI functions.

There is, though, an inherent equality within a COPI; value of participation is not determined by the number of times an individual contributes to the dialogue. One may be silent throughout the majority of an inquiry or, indeed, throughout a series of inquiries, but that participant is thinking and following the argument and will ultimately take away what was said to his/her life outside the community and he/she has the potential to change in some way as a result of the inquiry or reflection upon it after the session has ended. Not only has the individual the potential to change as a result of the inquiry, he/she has the potential to change the environment, institutions and other individuals around him/her. 'The COPI assumes that at any one instant any person, child or adult, might have an insight of great value to contribute. . . . There is an assumption of equality of people in a strong sense' (McCall, 1991, p. 31). Unfortunately there has not yet been a documented COPI where children and adults are within one group or community. There is a case for keeping them separate in that the children *perhaps* do not have the breadth of vocabulary available to some older people or the experience to understand some of the examples used. However, with regard to sharing concepts, ideas or opinions, there is no reason why groups should not be comprised of individuals from a range of ages as well as social backgrounds. This is something well worth considering in the event of citizens' juries, although from a practical perspective, the physical organization would best be facilitated in separate groupings since children are in educational institutions throughout the day, then it would be easier to manage logistically that their sessions occur throughout the course of the school day. Morrison *et al.* suggest that 'In developing new means by which children can be heard, politicians should themselves find more effective, appropriate ways of communicating with children/young people, providing opportunities for them to participate directly in debate and decision making' (2000, p. 7) and COPI may just be the way to provide for this – although it cannot be tokenistic, action must be taken based upon the young people's input. It is important that young people are not only encouraged to inquire and inquire in depth, but that this be facilitated for them in order that they can challenge received wisdom and develop their own beliefs, for as Siegel (1988) suggests:

> Students, in short, are indoctrinated if they are led to hold beliefs in such a way that they are prevented from critically inquiring into their legitimacy and the power of the evidence offered in their support; if

they hold beliefs in such a way that the beliefs are not open to rational evaluation and assessment.

(Siegel, 1988, p. 80)

This is precisely why a practice such as COPI is useful for all members of our society, individuals should be aware that everything is open to question.

While it is vital that society members question and inquire through the sharing of ideas and opinions in a Community of Inquiry, the only issue here may be, if one wishes to use the dialogue as a means for change in the society and the community, that it is difficult (if not impossible) to ascertain exactly how the individual feels, or what he/she personally holds as it is the case that he/she is able to offer ideas not as personally held beliefs which will be contributions to the dialogue and also bearing in mind that the inquiry does not seek a consensus or conclusion. However, the COPI could be the place where citizens – of whatever age – are trained and practised in their reasoning skills while also taking part in citizens' juries which may follow a similar format, but one whereby decisions or individual conclusions may be reached in order that action may be taken – having been informed through the argumentation skills inherited from the COPI. Additionally, the COPI is a useful place to air as many views as possible in order that individuals have perspectives to consider in formulating their personal standpoints in order to generate action. It is therefore not simply the promotion of a young individual's right to have his/her opinions or views heard – which is indeed a shift in the running of society – but all members of that society should be treated as citizens and should have an equal voice. Mill's *Utilitarianism* advocates just such an approach to equality,

... society between human beings ... is manifestly impossible on any other footing than that the interests of all are to be consulted. Society between equals can only exist on the understanding that the interests of all are to be regarded equally.

(Mill, 1972, p. 29)

The equality that exists in the COPI is one that society could borrow from, where *all* participants, of whatever age, are encouraged to reason, reflect and inquire. Indeed, Rousseau makes the very relevant point that 'If we do not form the habit of thinking as children, we shall lose the power of thinking for the rest of our life' (1948, p. 82). Siegel (1988) reinforces this idea that we desire for our community critical thinkers, individuals who are adept reasoners and who are receptive to the reasoning of others – this is what will shift society towards community, and this is what Community of Philosophical Inquiry aims to promote. Siegel sees critical thinking as an ability to reason and use such reasoning skills to justify

> ... beliefs, claims, and actions. A critical thinker, then, is one who is *appropriately moved by reasons*: she has a propensity or disposition to believe and act in accordance with reasons; and she has the ability properly to assess the force of reasons in the many contexts in which reasons play a role.
>
> (Siegel, 1988, p. 23)

Siegel's definition of a critical thinker does not preclude children.

Equal Persons

From her study of Firestone, Purdy suggests that 'If children were no longer separated from adult society, we cannot predict what they would be like. It is plausible to believe that they would, in general, behave more maturely and be happier to boot' (1998, p. 199). This takes us back to the medieval period discussed earlier, that children were not set apart from adults and were privy to all conversations and activities – with the notable exception of decision-making. However, the ordinary 'man/woman on the street' was not at that time involved in the decision-making process either. Being a child is, it seems, that time when decisions are taken for us because it is believed that we cannot contribute as citizens. Yet, there are older society members for whom this is also the case, for instance, those

suffering from a mental illness. Even prisoners in criminal institutions are not permitted to play a part in the decision-making
process, and although they are not called children, it is often
acknowledged that they are treated *like* children. If we think back
to the earlier discussion on *person*, it was suggested that prisoners
have their personhood stripped from them as a punishment, but
that they must be treated *as* persons in order for those outwith the
institution, the policy makers, judge, jury and general public, to
remain persons in their own right. What is the implication, then,
for children or younger members of our society?

Certainly they must, like the prisoners, be treated as persons for
the sake of the personhood of the caregivers and they are persons in
their own right because this is a given status at birth. So, perhaps
the question of personhood is not an issue, but that of citizenhood,
for that is what allows one to participate in society, and as yet
children are not perceived of or treated as citizens. A voice is now
being given to them, but not in any formal manner on a regular
basis and this opportunity to raise ideas or opinions appears still to
be seen as a *preparation* for citizenhood when one is an adult. It
should also be noted that we talk of 'giving' children a voice. It is
important that we are wary of *giving* children a voice; they should
be able to speak out for themselves, a forum and means should be
created for such a thing to happen to avoid an adult mouthpiece
stating children's opinions under his/her own interpretation. A
much more inclusive society – a community perhaps – is needed
where all individuals have a platform to speak from and be heard in
order that their views may influence policy and practice. As
deWinter (1997) suggests,

> If children are actively committed to community development, this
> will yield them more power. But they gain an equally important
> learning experience: we count, we are taken seriously, our ideas are
> appreciated, our environment evidently also belongs to us and
> therefore it is worth making an effort for. In other words: participation
> by children and young people is a way of enlarging the influence of the
> young on their own living situation and living environment, but it is
> also a way of shaping and strengthening their commitment to society
>   (deWinter, 1997, p. 43)

and, I would hold, community. Children, then, appear to be con-strained by their social status. In *Emile* Rousseau holds that 'There can be no society without exchange, no exchange without a com-mon standard of measurement, no common standard of measure-ment without equality. Hence the first law of every society is some conventional equality either in men or things' (1948, p. 152) – and here, children are the 'things' that need to be made equal. This highlights the need to redefine the boundaries of childhood. Madge sees this as changing and recognizes the inequality in status, 'Children are not regarded as apprentice adults but as a social group in their own right. While they will not be children forever, their status in childhood does not rest on the fact that they will one day become adults' (2006, p. 2).

Yes, children should be afforded protection from harm by the State, but then, so should all individuals. Yes, children's voices should be taken account of in decision and policy-making, but then, so should the voices of all individuals who are citizens. Yes, children should have rights, but they too are bound by obligations like the older members of our society; and not all adult obligations are the same or equal, since not everyone lives in the same envir-onment or under the same set of circumstances. Likewise, the obligations that younger individuals take on need not be the same as each other or those belonging to the older members of society.

Turner (1998) cites Robson and Robson and links children with women in one respect, and then separates them in another:

> ... the classing together ... of women and children, appears to me both indefensible in principle and mischievous in practice. Children below a certain age cannot judge or act for themselves; up to a con-siderably greater age they are inevitably more or less disqualified for doing so; but women are as capable as men of appreciating and managing their own concerns, and the only hindrance to their doing so arises from the injustice of their present social position.
>
> (Turner, 1998, p. 139)

Turner sees the link that both children and women are unequal in the world of power, yet she fails to see that like women, children are disenfranchized, but she raises the point that children cannot judge for themselves. The argument links closely to that of children being seen as pre-rational beings. Children can and do judge their actions and the actions of others and Darling recognizes that it is *expected* behaviours that are talked about when considering children's role or status in society: 'Our assumptions today about appropriate behaviour *for* children, and about appropriate behaviour *towards* children can sometimes be most clearly identified when long-established behavioural patterns are seen to be broken' (2000, p. 1). He continues by asking an important question, one that does not take account of children having a moral code of their own which society has yet to shape to coincide with the accepted and ruling moral code; he asks

> . . . why murder perpetrated by a child should require an enquiry of a kind seldom triggered by murder by an adult. The answer surely lies in the conviction that childhood is a time of innocence, badness is acquired later. In the early stages of a human being's existence, innocence is the natural condition: it is lost through exposure to an imperfect society.
>
> (*ibid.*, p. 2)

There are several points at issue here.

In answer to Darling's initial question, an enquiry is possibly held because our current society does not perceive children as being capable of reasoning about an action such as murder, that they may not see it as wrong because their moral code, in such an instance, has not been bent into the accepted shape of the majority. The child murderer may not be fully aware of the consequences incurred in society by perpetrating a murder, unlike his/her adult counterpart who has been fully inducted into the 'acceptable' modes of being in a society which may mean that the young murderer lacks the experience which informs one of the results of such an act that may, in fact, be the deterrent the older potential murderer has. Secondly, childhood is perhaps not so much the period of innocence that Darling suggests, but rather a time when one is coming to terms with one's obligations and is learning the accepted behaviour patterns and experience has not yet demonstrated to the child all that is on offer, thus preserving 'innocence' by not making available vices or opportunities which will later become much more evident. One may add to this that 'badness' is not so much acquired later as perhaps *attributed* later – the new member of society must learn what society perceives as being bad or wrong, which may (or may not) conflict with his/her own moral code. Mayo asserts that morality is not merely a way of behaving but is, in actual fact, a way of *thinking* about behaving. He says that 'Morality necessarily involves moral thinking as well as moral action' (1986, p. 8) and this is yet another feature or attribute children are considered not to possess. However, Community of Philosophical Inquiry disproves this as time and time again children within a COPI will discuss – at very deep philosophical levels – moral issues and dilemmas. Finally, as to Darling's suggestion that it is the 'imperfect society' which alters the innocence of the young, certainly experience of society perhaps alters the child and his/her 'innocence', but the notion of an '*imperfect*' society remains to be defined. Society can only be what its members make it and for it to be perfect implies that everyone is the same, will be the same and will share the same ideas, that it is static – this cannot be the case. Mill (1985) links childhood and old age together in the way that society treats individuals:

> Society has had absolute power over them during all the early portion of their existence; it has had the whole period of childhood and nonage in which to try whether it could make them capable of rational conduct in life.
>
> (Mill, 1985, p. 149)

It is, in fact, some form of social construction and power which determines what a child is, not what his/her role should be.

Darling (2000) suggests that

> In societies where you are seen as an adult when you are ten, then you *are* an adult when you are ten. Here we surely have a striking illustration of the power of perceptions to create a corresponding reality:

where young people are assumed to be capable of bearing responsibility, they are given adult responsibility; and the experience of being treated in this way contributes to the development of a responsible nature.

(Darling, 2000, p. 17)

Defining Child

So, it would appear that adulthood is the preserve of responsibility and obligations, but then, younger individuals bear this load also. How, then, do we define what a child *is*? Gillett (1987) maintains that

Human beings are born with a certain constitution and, through the many and varied experiences that they undergo, develop into adults with a certain conceptual repertoire, character, set of memories, self-image, emotionality, aspirations, abilities, eccentricities, and so on, all of which are holistically interconnected ... Our concepts and thoughts have meaning in so far as we acquire and use them within this process of maturation. The nature of this process and the complex interrelation between personal history, brain structure, and mental function means that a person cannot simply be replicated, replaced, or divided. Both personal identity and mental ascriptions are determined within a framework of these conditions.

(Gillett, 1987, p. 80)

Gillett is misled, as are the other thinkers who have tried to define child in terms of becoming, developing, evolving or growing into adulthood. We have seen that adults have a consciousness, an awareness. We have seen that adults are rational beings and can reason. We have seen that adults are perceived of as being persons. We have seen that adults have moral codes and can discern right from wrong and good from bad. We have seen that adults participate in society as citizens. We have seen that adults have a self which shapes their identity and continues throughout one's life. A child does not vote, does not work, does not earn, does not drive, marry or contribute to policy-making decisions – yet there are many of those beyond 18 (the age set down by the UN) that do not do these things either. We can, it seems, only negatively define what a child is – we can say what it is *not*, but at the same time, it has a role function within society, one that is a control or power enabler, one that ensures the status quo is maintained.

Children perhaps question too much; Morgan states that 'Once the child has learned the meaning of "why" and "because", he has become a fully paid up member of the human race' (1996, p. 137). Perhaps adults do not want children to question and reason because in taking account of their views, ideas and opinions they may have to alter their own. Childhood could be seen as a period of indoctrination, the time when young humans become less animal or instinctual and learn how one is expected to be in society. Yet now that government and society's educators are talking in terms of Citizenship Education, a more participative model of society is required – we are breeding citizens, but this begins when young; individuals have their reasoning skills facilitated and honed in order that they may contribute to the emergent community – once more the boundaries of child/adult are becoming blurred. Like the COPI, individuals are important, but individuals *as* individuals, not because they possess a certain age or status. Community of Philosophical Inquiry is a positive model for our society and how the younger members of that society are treated.

Archard posits that 'Childhood could ... be understood simply as the absence of adult qualities' (1993, p. 36). This is not the case, the child is *not* an adult without certain qualities or attributes; the point that has been missed until now is that an adult is a child *plus* more of the qualities and attributes that Gillett gave to adults. Children have the things that Gillett attributes to adults; they have '... a conceptual repertoire, character, set of memories, self-image, emotionality, aspirations, abilities and eccentricities' (1987, p. 80), there is nothing here listed that is the preserve of adult, biologically mature human beings. Children, in this instance, may be compared – loosely – with a car. The child is the basic model; it has a chassis, an engine, steering wheel, gears, wheels and all the other facets that make the car roadworthy and fit for its purpose. One may add to the basic model; the car may soon have included in its make-up a CD player, a navigational system, alloy wheels and drinks holders. It is in this way that children are like adults – the child is the basic model, fully functioning and effective and as time or experience passes more functions or aptitudes are able to be employed more readily. It is *not* that the child is missing these functions, aptitudes, skills or abilities in the first place – and this is where the consideration of children has gone awry – it is that some individuals as they are more involved in the world of things acquire these new or more developed or evolved attributes, skills, aptitudes and abilities. It may not be the case necessarily that because of one's age one has more gadgets and tools at one's disposal like the accessorized car; some individuals will extend their devices as they age and others will not. It is the mistake of society that behaves as though those who are more mature in years automatically become entitled to be treated like the highly specified sports car. The child, as a concept, is no different in essence to the adult.

In keeping the category 'child' we, adults, are establishing the power structures within our society and are setting limits on who can participate and in what ways they may participate. Qvortrup *et al.* (1994) highlight this point,

> The relationship between adults and children is therefore most likely not regulated philosophically, but by power and interests. If children are treated differently from adults the reason is not that they are not active, but that they are not active in the way in which adults are active. This means that the adult world does not recognize children's praxis, because competence is defined merely in relation to adults' praxis – a suggestion which is all the more powerful since adults are in a sovereign position to define competence.
>
> (Qvortrup *et al.*, 1994, p. 4)

It is this issue of how we involve children – or individuals who fall into this category – in our society in a participative manner which is of importance.

Conclusions

It has been suggested that through Community of Philosophical Inquiry children would be promoted in the social sphere and would become more equal members of society and the community created by the sense of common purpose engendered by such a practice. At present children are given a voice within society only in terms of what adults want to relate and even then it is through the mouths of adults that we come to hear what adults think children are saying or interpret them as saying. The world of the child is one which is closely controlled and monitored, their lives are time-tabled and barriers are put in the way of their enjoying the opportunities or experiences afforded to adult members of society. Children are expected to be innocent and receptive individuals – this is the role they are expected to play and while in this role they are trained into the model of the 'acceptable' adult. What is needed, it has been claimed here, is that children are in need of empowerment – ironically the empowerment can only be given by adults; they should be encouraged to be citizens, they should be given opportunities to explore the issues that impact upon their lives and the lives of the wider society, they should have their own voices and have a place in society where these voices may be heard and have notice taken of them. The voices of children, and equally those of adults, should not exist in isolation where everyone is free to expound their thoughts and theories, what is important is that a sense of community is created and that what people – adults and children – see as important is that there is dialogue and it is this dialogue which can and will effect change. Kennedy (2006) maintains that

> ... as children are progressively accorded the status of full-fledged interlocutors with adults, that space will bloom in ways that have been characteristically suppressed until now, and the human experience will, however slowly, change to allow ... as Samuel Taylor Coleridge put it ... each of us to 'carry the feelings of childhood into the powers of manhood'.
>
> (Kennedy, 2006, p. 25)

One way in which change could be facilitated is through providing the tools for effective dialogue where critical reasoning is encouraged and the tools for such reason and reflection are practised through Community of Philosophical Inquiry.

Conclusion

The aim of this book has been to come to some acceptable definition of the concept of 'child'. From the outset it has been evident that a child human being and an adult human being are different types of the same thing – although this has not always been the case. With the advent of childhood as a social phenomenon in the late seventeenth and early eighteenth centuries, the division between adults and children has grown, although in recent years there appears to have been a return to the medieval treatment or perception of younger human beings and the division between the two groups is becoming more blurred and less defined. Part of the reason for this increasing lack of definition is linked to society and the role children have within such a context.

In order to determine what exactly a child *is*, it has been necessary to establish in what ways human beings differ from the rest of the animal kingdom. Not only is it the case that humans do not act on every impulse they have, the manner in which they respond and act towards others in their social group sets them apart from the 'beasts'. Those that behave in such a way as to treat others as ends in themselves and not merely as a means to an end were given the label – or role – person. Personhood is an attribute given at birth on the understanding that if one could one would treat others as ends in themselves – as persons. Therefore, children are treated *as* persons, but as yet they will not have had the opportunity to treat others as persons. It was also shown that person is a role concept, one which has expected behaviours built-in which relate to our moral codes and treating others as ends in themselves. As human animals we are social creatures and as persons we agree to abide by the rules established within our society.

It is being claimed that we each individually have a moral code in the sense that there are actions and ideas which resonate with us as being right or wrong, good or bad. We have a conscience which enables us to determine how we feel about things in terms of their rightness or wrongness – animals do not appear to have this faculty. As we are all individuals with an individual make-up it cannot be expected that we will all share the same moral code. What is being suggested is that there are certain areas upon which moral codes will concur and the majority moral code will be the one set as the accepted manner of behaving or conducting oneself in society. In accepting the role of person within a society one is also agreeing to abide by the rules set by the majority moral code. This does not necessarily imply that the majority moral code goes unquestioned or challenged; in fact, it is a duty of all citizens to critically reflect upon the running of one's society. As Villa suggests, Socrates' '... essential task is to get his fellow Athenians to entertain the possibility that the demands of morality may, in fact, run counter to the established norms of the society and its conception of virtuous citizenship' (2001, p. 3). Building upon this, while it has been posited that we are all equipped with a moral code, children are more often than not perceived as possessing little in the manner of a moral code, or at least one that is likely to be accepted by the holders of power within society – adults. Children are therefore socialized into an accepted mode of being. Their moral codes may be manipulated and moulded into what is 'appropriate' for a particular society if we ignore Socrates' goal.

This moulding and socializing of the younger members of society links strongly with the ways in which we have defined person. Children are perceived of as in a permanent state of *becoming*. It has been argued that in treating children in this way they are not persons since they are not being treated as ends in themselves but as a means to an end – as a future adult. We may say that children are treated not as human *beings* but as human *becomings*. Additionally, the discussion of the notion of self demonstrated, that children possess selves, that these selves go some way to shaping the identity of an individual; the self is the internal device which works to interpret the external world. It is important to recall that the idea that one can only have a self at the end of a complete lifetime was refuted as there would be little, if any point, in there being a self if this was the case. As the self is a processor which works for the creation of the I and, as it is a constant within one's life in that it maintains part of the continuity of one's personal identity, then one cannot suddenly acquire a self at the age of eighteen when the United Nations determines that one is an adult. No, one must be born with a self since it must begin to interpret the physical world from the moment one becomes conscious or aware.

The physical world of which one is conscious is a world constituted of and by moral issues. Children are not, cannot, and should not be abstracted from this realm. This moral space is one inhabited by citizens. Citizens are those working for the betterment of the society in which they live. They are active participants in their society or community and this active participation is political. The political action of a citizen is made effective by the fact that to be a truly effective citizen one should be a reasoning and reflective individual. However, while one is a reasoning and critically reflective individual one does not undertake this reflection or appraisal in isolation, as an individual. It has been claimed in this work that in order for a fully functioning citizenry to exist there must be *dialogue*. Saran *et al.* suggest that Socratic Dialogue engenders citizen behaviour, '. . . Socratic Dialogue enables ordinary people to philosophise with the aim of enriching and informing civic life' (2004b, p. 1). This openness to all is crucial. Dialogue should be open to all in an egalitarian format where there is space for everyone to speak, be heard and feel their input is valued and has some bearing on the future policy-making of one's society. The notion of citizens' juries is a positive one and one which may easily be made available to all members of society. Children are not outwith society although this is the manner in which they are often treated with adults making decisions for them and controlling their lives in a great variety of ways from the clothes they wear and food they eat to the age at which they are legally allowed to leave school or begin having sexual intercourse. Children should have their own voices heard; they should be encouraged and empowered to participate as citizens in their society in order that they work with the other members of that society for its improvement. Madge suggests that 'Children are participants in structuring the social order, and this becomes apparent when their voices are heard' (2006, p. 2). Children could easily participate in citizens' juries. What has been suggested in this book is that while citizens' juries are a useful tool, the practice of Community of Philosophical Inquiry (COPI) may be a positive model or structure under which dialogue could take place.

In the discussion on the practice of COPI it was held that within the practice there are some fundamental principles governing its nature. First, the practice assumes that as human beings we are all fallible, secondly, that we are all creative and thirdly, that we all, as humans, have the capacity to reason. COPI is egalitarian also in that no individual within the dialogue is set apart as an authority, all contributions are regarded equally although some may develop the dialogue further than others. Over time the members of a COPI will become less possessive of their contributions, they will come to view the dialogue as more important than ownership of an individual idea; this search for meaning or a deeper understanding is the common purpose or goal of the Community of Philosophical Inquiry. The practice is one which does not alter in terms of structure – and often content – with different participants. COPI is a practice that works in the same way no matter whether the participants have experience of COPI lasting five or ten years or if they are a beginning group or if the participants are adults or children – the structure of Community of Philosophical Inquiry remains constant regardless of the experience or age of its participants. The assumption is that *everyone* has the capacity to reason.

Claims by developmental psychologists such as Piaget have been refuted in this work. While such thinkers hold that children are incapable of being reasoning and reflective individuals, that they are in some way non-rational or pre-rational, it is through the work of Matthews, Lipman and more especially McCall that it can be seen that children are perfectly capable of critical thinking and reasoning. Contrary to the notion that such thinking in children is merely 'romancing', COPI demonstrates that children are able to listen, reflect, counter and build upon the reasoning and arguments of others. In fact, very often children are much more adept at building arguments from the ideas of others than are adults; there is less of a sense of ownership of individual ideas. A Community of Philosophical Inquiry composed entirely of children works hard to develop the theme of the dialogue rather than trying to win over support or form firm conclusions. COPI with children is an extremely positive model of how loyalty to a dialogue and a search for meaning may be shared and used for the betterment of its participants without a concern for winning points and trying to gain some kind of status. This is the way in which children could be more involved as active, participating, political citizens. One need not be concerned about involving children in society as political citizens since they have opinions and ideas which reflect and relate to society. Also, through such a practice thinking and reflecting individuals are encouraged, and through practise and over time individuals may become more reflective, reasoning and critical citizens who will be less inclined to accept unquestioningly what they are told and an overall promotion of working for a common cause will be engendered.

It is not that children and adults are so different; it is that until *now* the discussion about children has been the wrong way round. Children have been viewed from a 'complete' adult perspective; they have been seen in terms of what they will *become*. When children are discussed they are talked about as lacking reason, as lacking any moral sense, as having no responsibilities or duties, as future adults, as citizens in the making, in other words, as a means to an end. It is not the case that children are adults minus qualities x, y and z; rather, children *are*. Children are, and adults are children *plus* x, y and z, where x, y and z are not necessarily reasoning abilities, personhood or citizenship. No, children are persons, they can and do reason, they do have opinions and should be given the space for those voices to be heard, they do have moral codes and sensibilities, they do have responsibilities and they could be citizens given the opportunity. It is, in fact, the older members of society who keep children in their place and ensure they learn their place – one of becoming. If children were enfranchized members of society, they too could be active, political, critical and effective citizens working for the benefit of all in generating a community. One of the ways this may be promoted is through the practice of Community of Philosophical Inquiry as a tool for dialogue on a deep and reflective level. It is within Community of Philosophical Inquiry that children are treated as persons. It is in Community of Philosophical Inquiry that they are perceived of as reasoning and rational individuals. And it is in Community of Philosophical Inquiry that we move towards a more egalitarian notion of individuals rather than perpetrating the divide of adult and child.

Bibliography

Archambault, R. D. (1966), *Dewey on Education: Appraisals*. New York: Random House Incorporated.

Archard, D. (1993), *Children: Rights and Childhood*. London: Routledge.

Archard, D. (1998), 'John Locke's children', in: S. M. Turner and G. B. Matthews (eds), *The Philosopher's Child: Critical Perspectives in the Western Tradition*. Rochester, NY: University of Rochester Press.

Ariès, P. (1996), *Centuries of Childhood*. London: Pimlico.

Aristotle. (1955), *Ethics*. London: Penguin Books Limited.

Aristotle. (1986), *De Anima (On the soul)*. London: Penguin Books Limited.

Atkins, P. (1987), 'Purposeless people', in: A. Peacocke and G. Gillett (eds), *Persons and Personality*. Oxford: Basil Blackwell Limited.

Barthes, R. (1982), 'Toys', in C. Jenks (ed.), *The Sociology of Childhood: Essential Readings*. London: Batsford Academic and Educational Limited.

Barthes, R. (1993), *Mythologies*. London: Vintage Books.

Becker, L. C. (1998), 'Stoic children', in S. M. Turner and G.B. Matthews (eds), *The Philosopher's Child: Critical Perspectives in the Western Tradition*. Rochester, NY: University of Rochester Press.

Bellamy, C. (1996), 'Foreword', in S. Jeleff (ed.), *The Child as Citizen*. Strasbourg: Council of Europe Publishing.

Bonnett, M. (1994), *Children's Thinking: Promoting Understanding in the Primary School*. London: Cassell.

Bourdieu, P. (2001), *Language and Symbolic Power*. Cambridge, Massachusetts: Harvard University Press.

Boyden, J. (1997), 'Childhood and the policy makers: a comparative perspective on the globalization of childhood', in A. James and A. Prout (eds), *Constructing and Reconstructing Childhood: Contemporary Issues in the Sociological Study of Childhood*. London: Falmer Press.

Brennan, S. and Noggle, R. (1998), 'John Rawls's children', in S. M. Turner and G.B. Matthews (eds), *The Philosopher's Child: Critical Perspectives in the Western Tradition*. Rochester, NY: University of Rochester Press.

Cassidy, C. (2006a), 'Child and Community of Philosophical Inquiry', in *Childhood and Philosophy: Journal of the International Council of Philosophical Inquiry with Children*, 2(4). www.filoeduc.org/childphilo/n4/Claire Cassidy.htm

Cassidy, C. (2006b), 'Children: Animals or Persons?', in *Thinking: Journal of Philosophy for Children*, 17(3).

Cartledge, P. (2002), *Becoming a Citizen: Then and Now*. Roberts Lecture delivered at Dickinson College, Carlisle, Pennsylvania.

Centore, F. F. (1979), *Persons, a Comparative Account of the Six Possible Theories*. Westport, Connecticut: Greenwood Press Incorporated.

Claydon, L. F. (1969), *Rousseau on Education*. London: Collier-Macmillan Limited.

Connor, S. (1997), 'The modern auditory I', in R. Porter (ed.), *Rewriting the Self: Histories from the Renaissance to the Present*. London: Routledge.

Cunningham, H. (1995), *Children and Childhood in Western Society Since 1500*. London: Longman.

Cunningham, H. (2006), *The Invention of Childhood*. London: BBC Books.

Darling, J. (2000), *How We See Children: the Legacy of Rousseau's Emile*. Aberdeen: University of Aberdeen, Centre for Educational Research; 2000.

Delanty, G. (2003), *Community*. London: Routledge.

deMause, L., (ed.) (1995a), *The History of Childhood*. Northvale, NJ: Jason Aronson Incorporated.

deMause, L. (1995b), 'The evolution of childhood', in L. deMause (ed.), *The History of Childhood*. Northvale, NJ: Jason Aronson Incorporated.

Dennett, D. C. (1976), 'Conditions of personhood', in A.O. Rorty (ed.), *The Identities of Persons*. Berkeley: University of California Press.

Dennett, D. C. (1993), *Consciousness Explained*. London: Penguin Books Limited.

Denzin, N. K. (1982), 'The work of little children', in C. Jenks (ed.), *The Sociology of Childhood: Essential Readings*. London: Batsford Academic and Educational Limited.

deSousa, R. (1976), 'Rational homunculi', in A.O. Rorty (ed.), *The Identities of Persons*. Berkeley: University of California Press.

Dewey, J. (1963), *Experience and Education*. London: Collier-Macmillan Limited.

deWinter, M. (1997), *Children as Fellow Citizens: Participation and Commitment*. Oxford: Radcliffe Medical Press Limited.

Donaldson, M. (1978), *Children's Minds*. London: Fontana Press.

Downie, R. S. (1971), *Roles and Values*. London: Methuen & Company Limited.

Downie, R. S. and Telfer, E. (1969), *Respect for Persons*. London: George Allen & Unwin Limited.

Drew, S. (2000), *Children and the Human Rights Act 1998*. London: Save the Children.

Durkheim, E. (1982), 'Childhood', in C. Jenks (ed.), *The Sociology of Childhood: Essential Readings*. London: Batsford Academic and Educational Limited.

Elkin, F. and Handel, G. (1978), *The Child and Society: the Process of Socialization*. New York: Random House.

Emmet, D. (1966), *Rules, Roles and Relations*. Basingstoke: MacMillan & Company Limited.

Ennew, J. (1994), 'Time for children or time for adults?', in J. Qvortrup, M. Bardy, G. Sgritta and H. Wintersberger (eds), *Childhood Matters: Social Theory, Practice and Politics*. Aldershot: Avebury.

Faulks, K. (2000), *Citizenship*. London: Routledge.

Foot, P. (ed.) (1967), *Theories of Ethics*. London: Oxford University Press.

Frankfurt, H. (1976), 'Identification and externality', in A.O. Rorty (ed.), *The Identities of Persons*. Berkeley: University of California Press.

Frones, I. (1994), 'Dimensions of childhood', in J. Qvortrup, M. Bardy, G. Sgritta and H. Wintersberger (eds), *Childhood Matters: Social Theory, Practice and Politics*. Aldershot: Avebury.

Giddens, A. (1993), *Sociology*. Cambridge: Polity Press.

Gillett, G. (1987), 'Reasoning about persons', in A. Peacocke and G. Gillett (eds), *Persons and Personality*. Oxford: Basil Blackwell Limited.

Giroux, H. A. (1981), *Ideology, Culture and the Process of Schooling*. Philadelphia: Temple University Press.

Gittins, D. (2004), 'The historical construction of childhood', in M. J. Kehily (ed.), *An Introduction to Childhood Studies*. Maidenhead: Open University Press.

Harre, R. (1987), 'Persons and selves', in A. Peacocke and G. Gillett (eds), *Persons and Personality*. Oxford: Basil Blackwell Limited.

Hendrick, H. (1997), 'Constructions and reconstructions of British childhood: an interpretative survey, 1800 to the present', in: A. James and A. Prout (eds), *Constructing and Reconstructing Childhood: Contemporary Issues in the Sociological Study of Childhood*. London: Falmer Press.

Herzlich, C. (1973), *Health and Illness*. London: Academic Press Incorporated (London) Limited.

Hillman, J. (1982), 'Abandoning the child', in C. Jenks (ed.), *The Sociology of Childhood: Essential Readings*. London: Batsford Academic and Educational Limited.

Hobbes, T. (1949), *De Cive; or, the Citizen*. New York: Appleton-Century-Crofts, Incorporated.

Hofstadter, D. R. and Dennett, D.C. (eds) (1982), *The Mind's I*. London: Penguin Books.

Hume, D. (1975), *Enquiries Concerning Human Understanding and Concerning the Principles of Morals*. Oxford: Oxford University Press.

Hundert, E. J. (1997), 'The European enlightenment and the history of the self', in R. Porter (ed.), *Rewriting the Self: Histories of the Renaissance to the Present*. London: Routledge.

Hunt, P. (2004), 'Children's literature and childhood', in M. J. Kehily (ed.), *An Introduction to Childhood Studies*. Maidenhead: Open University Press.

Hunter. G. (ed) (1994), *Spinoza: the Enduring Questions*. Toronto: University of Toronto Press Incorporated.

James, A., Jenks, C. and Prout, A. (1998), *Theorizing Childhood*. Cambridge: Polity Press.

James, A. and Prout, A. (eds) (1997a), *Constructing and Reconstructing Childhood: Contemporary Issues in the Sociological Study of Childhood*. London: Falmer Press.

James, A. and Prout, A. (1997b), 'Re-presenting childhood: time and transition in the study of childhood', in A. James and A. Prout (eds), *Constructing and Reconstructing Childhood: Contemporary Issues in the Sociological Study of Childhood*. London: Falmer Press.

Jeffreys, M. V. C. (1967), *John Locke, Prophet of Common Sense*. London: Methuen and Company Limited.

Jeleff, S. (ed.) (1996), *The Child as Citizen*. Strasbourg: Council of Europe Publishing.

Jenks, C. (1982a), 'Constituting the child', in C. Jenks (ed.), *The Sociology of*

Childhood: Essential Readings. London: Batsford Academic and Educational Limited.

Jenks, C. (ed.) (1982b), *The Sociology of Childhood: Essential Readings*. London: Batsford Academic and Educational Limited.

Jenks, C. (1996), *Childhood*. London: Routledge.

Jenks, C. (2004), 'Constructing childhood sociologically', in M. J. Kehily (ed.), *An Introduction to Childhood Studies*. Maidenhead: Open University Press.

Joad, C. E. M. (1957), *Guide to Philosophy*. New York: Dover Publications.

Kant, I. (1989), *Groundwork of the Metaphysic of Morals*. London: Unwin Hyman Limited.

Kehily, M. J. (ed.) (2004a), *An Introduction to Childhood Studies*. Maidenhead: Open University Press.

Kehily, M. J. (2004b), 'Understanding childhood: an introduction to some key themes and issues', in M. J. Kehily (ed.), *An Introduction to Childhood Studies*. Maidenhead: Open University Press.

Kennedy, D. (2006), *The Well of Being: Childhood, Subjectivity and Education*. Albany: State University of New York Press.

King, P.O. (1998), 'Thomas Hobbes's children', in S. M. Turner and G.B. Matthews (eds), *The Philosopher's Child: Critical Perspectives in the Western Tradition*. Rochester, NY: University of Rochester Press.

Law, S. (2006), *The War for Children's Minds*. Abingdon: Routledge.

Lawson, H. (2001), *Active Citizenship in Schools and the Community*. London: Routledge.

Lewis, D. (1976), 'Survival and identity', in A.O. Rorty (ed.), *The Identities of Persons*. Berkeley: University of California Press.

Lindfors, J.W. (1999), *Children's Inquiry: Using Language to Make Sense of the World*. New York, NY: Teachers College, Columbia University Press.

Lipman, M. (1988), *Philosophy Goes to School*. Philadelphia: Temple University Press.

Lipman, M. (1991), *Thinking in Education*. Cambridge: Cambridge University Press.

Locke, J. (1976), *An Essay Concerning Human Understanding*. London: J.M. Dent and Sons Limited.

Lyman Jr., R. B. (1995), 'Barbarianism and religion: late Roman and early medieval childhood', in L. deMause (ed.), *The History of Childhood*. Northvale, NJ: Jason Aronson Incorporated.

MacIntyre, A. (1999), *After Virtue*. London: Gerald Duckworth & Company Limited.

MacMurray, J. (1969), *The Self as Agent*. London: Faber & Faber Limited.

MacMurray, J. (1970), *Persons in Relation*. London: Faber & Faber Limited.

Macquarrie, J. (1972), *Existentialism*. London: Hutchinson.

Madge, N. (2006), *Children These Days*. Bristol: The Policy Press.

Magee, B and Burnyeat, M. (1987), *The Great Philosophers*. London: BBC Books.

Mandeville, B. (1970), *The Fable of the Bees*. Harmondsworth: Pelican Books Limited.

Matthews, G.B. (1980), *Philosophy and the Young Child*. Cambridge, Massachusetts: Harvard University Press.

Matthews, G. B. (1984), *Dialogues with Children*. Cambridge, Massachusetts: Harvard University Press.

Matthews, G.B. (1994), *The Philosophy of Childhood*. Cambridge, Massachusetts: Harvard University Press.

Matthews, G.B. (1998), 'Socrates' children', in S.M. Turner and G. B. Matthews (eds), *The Philosopher's Child: Critical Perspectives in the Western Tradition*. Rochester, NY: University of Rochester Press; 1998.

Mayo, B. (1986), *The Philosophy of Right and Wrong*. London: Routledge & Kegan Paul Incorporated.

McCall, C. (1990), *Concepts of Person: an Analysis of Concepts of Person, Self and Human Being*. Aldershot: Avebury.

McCall, C. (1991), *Stevenson Lectures on Citizenship*. Glasgow: Glasgow University Press.

McCall, C. (1993), *Laura and Paul*. Glasgow: Glasgow University Press.

McGowan Tress, D. (1998), 'Aristotle's children', in S. M. Turner and G.B. Matthews (eds), *The Philosopher's Child: Critical Perspectives in the Western Tradition*. Rochester, NY: University of Rochester Press.

McLaughlin, M. M. (1995), 'Survivors and surrogates: children and parents from the 9th to 13th centuries', in L. deMause (ed.), *The History of Childhood*. Northvale, NJ: Jason Aronson Incorporated.

Meadows, S. (1983), *Developing Thinking*. London: Methuen and Company Limited.

Meadows, S. (1993), *The Child as Thinker*. London: Routledge.

Mill, J. S. (1972), *Utilitarianism, On Liberty and Considerations on Representative Government*. London: J.M. Dent & Sons.

Mill, J. S. (1985), *On Liberty*. London: Penguin Books.

Morgan, E. (1996), *The Descent of the Child: Human Evolution from a New Perspective*. London: Penguin Books.

Morrison, C. and McCulloch, C. (2000), *All Children, All Ages: the NGO*

Alternative Report (Scotland) to the UN Committee on the Rights of the Child. Edinburgh: Scottish Alliance for Children's Rights.

Morrison, J.C. (1994), 'Spinoza on the self, personal identity and immortality', in G. Hunter (ed.), *Spinoza: the Enduring Questions.* Toronto: University of Toronto Press Incorporated.

Moss, P. and Petrie, P. (2002), *From Children's Services to Children's Spaces: Public Policy, Children and Childhood.* London: Routledge Farmer.

Murdoch, I. (1953), *Sartre, Romantic Rationalist.* Cambridge: Bowes and Bowes.

Nagel, T. (1975), 'Brain bisection and the unity of consciousness', in J. Perry (ed.), *Personal Identity.* Berkeley: University of California Press.

Nagel, T. (1979), 'What is it like to be a bat?', in T. Nagel, *Mortal Questions.* Cambridge: Cambridge University Press.

Neville-Sington, P. and Sington, D. (1993), *Paradise Dreamed: How Utopian Thinkers Changed the Modern World.* London: Bloomsbury.

Newell, P. (1991), *The UN Convention and Children's Rights in the UK.* London: National Children's Bureau.

Noonan, H. (1991), *Personal Identity.* London: Routledge.

Norman, K. (1992), *Thinking Voices.* London: Hodder and Stoughton Limited.

Osler, A. (ed.) (2000), *Citizenship and Democracy in Schools: Diversity, Identity, Equality.* Stoke-on-Trent: Trentham Books Limited.

Parfit, D. (1976), 'Lewis, Perry and what matters', in A. O. Rorty (ed.), *The Identities of Persons.* Berkeley: University of California Press.

Parfit, D. (1984), *Reasons and Persons.* Oxford: Clarendon Press.

Parsons, T. (1982), 'The socialization of the child and the internalization of social value-orientations', in C. Jenks (ed.), *The Sociology of Childhood: Essential Readings.* London: Batsford Academic and Educational Limited.

Parsons, T. (2000), *Indeterminate Identity.* Oxford: Clarendon Press.

Peacocke, A. and Gillett, G. (eds) (1987), *Persons and Personality.* Oxford: Basil Blackwell Limited.

Penelhum, T. (1976), 'Self-identity and self-regard', in A.O. Rorty (ed.), *The Identities of Persons.* Berkeley: University of California Press.

Perkins, J. A. (1969), *The Concept of the Self in the French Enlightenment.* Geneva: Libraire Droz.

Perry, J. (ed.) (1975), *Personal Identity.* Berkeley: University of California Press.

Perry, J. (1976), 'The importance of being identical', in A. O. Rorty (ed.), *The Identities of Persons.* Berkeley: University of California Press.

Piaget, J. (1932), *The Moral Judgment of the Child*. London: Kegan, Paul, Trench, Trubner and Company Limited.

Piaget, J. (1960), *The Language and Thought of the Child*. London: Routledge and Kegan Paul Limited.

Piaget, J. (1971), *Science of Education and the Psychology of the Child*. Harlow: Longman Group Limited.

Piaget, J. (1974), *The Child and Reality: Problems of Genetic Psychology*. London: Frederick Muller Limited.

Plato. (1987a), *The Republic*. London: Penguin Books Limited.

Plato. (1987b), *Theaetetus*. London: Penguin Books Limited.

Porter, R. (ed.) (1997), *Rewriting the Self: Histories from the Renaissance to the Present*. London: Routledge.

Postman, N. (1994), *The Disappearance of Childhood*. New York: Vintage Books.

Pritchard, M. S. (1985), *Philosophical Adventures with Children*. Lanham, MD: University Press of America.

Prout, A. and James, A. (1997), 'A new paradigm for the sociology of childhood? Provenance, promise and problems', in A. James and A. Prout (eds), *Constructing and Reconstructing Childhood: Contemporary Issues in the Sociological Study of Childhood*. London: Falmer Press.

Pulaski, M. A. S. (1980), *Understanding Piaget: An Introduction to Children's Cognitive Development*. New York: Harper and Row.

Purdy, L. (1998), 'Shulamith Firestone's children', in S. M. Turner and G. B. Matthews (eds), *The Philosopher's Child: Critical Perspectives in the Western Tradition*. Rochester, NY: University of Rochester Press.

Quinton, A. (1975), 'The soul', in J. Perry (ed.), *Personal Identity*. Berkeley: University of California Press.

Qvortrup, J. (1997), 'A voice for children in statistical and social accounting: a plea for children's rights to be heard', in A. James and A. Prout (eds), *Constructing and Reconstructing Childhood: Contemporary Issues in the Sociological Study of Childhood*. London: Falmer Press.

Qvortrup, J., Bardy, M. Sgritta, G. and Wintersberger, H. (eds) (1994), *Childhood Matters: Social Theory, Practice and Politics*. Aldershot: Avebury.

Rachels, J. (1995), *The Elements of Moral Philosophy*. New York: McGraw-Hill Book Company.

Reid, T. (1969), *Essays on the Intellectual Powers of Man*. Massachusetts: M.I.T. Press.

Reid, T. (1975), 'Of Identity', in J. Perry (ed.), *Personal Identity*. Berkeley: University of California Press.

Richmond, P. G. (1970), *An Introduction to Piaget*. London: Routledge and Kegan Paul Limited.

Rorty, A. O. (1976a), 'A literary postscript: characters, persons, selves, individuals', in A.O. Rorty (ed.), *The Identities of Persons*. Berkeley: University of California Press.

Rorty, A.O. (ed.) (1976b), *The Identities of Persons*. Berkeley: University of California Press Limited.

Rose, N. (1997), 'Assembling the modern self', in R. Porter (ed.), *Rewriting the Self: Histories from the Renaissance to the Present*. London: Routledge.

Rosen, M. (ed.) (1995), *The Penguin Book of Childhood*. London: Penguin Books Limited.

Rousseau, J-J. (1948), *Emile or Education*. London: J.M. Dent and Sons Limited.

Rousseau, J-J. (1973), *The Social Contract and Discourses*. London: J.M. Dent and Sons Limited.

Rousseau, J-J. (1979), *The Reveries of a Solitary Walker*. New York: New York University Press.

Ruse, M. (1995), 'Human beings', in T. Honderich (ed.), *The Oxford Companion to Philosophy*. Oxford: Oxford University Press.

Saran, R. and Neisser, B. (eds) (2004a), *Enquiring Minds: Socratic Dialogue in Education*. Stoke-on-Trent: Trentham Books Limited.

Saran, R. and Neisser, B. (2004b), 'The Socratic Method and education: introduction', in R. Saran and B. Neisser (eds), *Enquiring Minds: Socratic Dialogue in Education*. Stoke-on-Trent: Trentham Books Limited.

Sartre, J. P. (1969), *Being and Nothingness*. London: Methuen and Company Limited.

Sawday, J. (1997), 'Self and selfhood in the seventeenth century', in R. Porter (ed.), *Rewriting the Self: Histories from the Renaissance to the Present*. London: Routledge.

Schneewind, J. B. (ed.) (1990a), *Moral Philosophy from Montaigne to Kant: An Anthology*. Volume 1. Cambridge: Cambridge University Press.

Schneewind, J. B. (ed.) (1990b), *Moral Philosophy from Montaigne to Kant: An Anthology*. Volume 2. Cambridge: Cambridge University Press.

Schrag, C. O. (1997), *The Self After Postmodernity*. New Haven: Yale University Press.

Schwebel, M. and Raph, J. (1974), *Piaget in the Classroom*. London: Routledge and Kegan Paul Limited.

Sedley, Rt.Hon. Lord Justice (2000), 'Foreword', in S. Drew, *Children and the Human Rights Act 1998*. London: Save the Children.

Shamgar-Handelman, L. (1994), 'To whom does childhood belong?', in J. Qvortrup, M. Bardy, G. Sgritta and H. Wintersberger (eds), *Childhood Matters: Social Theory, Practice and Politics*. Aldershot: Avebury.

Shaw, J. (1997), 'Formation of the early enlightenment self', in R. Porter (ed.), *Rewriting the Self: Histories from the Renaissance to the Present*. London: Routledge.

Shields, P. (1998), 'Ludwig Wittgenstein's children', in S. M. Turner and G. B. Matthews (eds), *The Philosopher's Child: Critical Perspectives in the Western Tradition*. Rochester, NY: University of Rochester Press.

Shoemaker, S. (1976), 'Embodiment and behavior', in A. O. Rorty (ed.), *The Identities of Persons*. Berkeley; University of California Press.

Siegel, H. (1988), *Educating Reason: Rationality, Critical Thinking and Education*. London: Routledge.

Simon, J. (1998), 'Jean-Jacques Rousseau's children', in S. M. Turner and G. B. Matthews (eds), *The Philosopher's Child: Critical Perspectives in the Western Tradition*. Rochester, NY: University of Rochester Press.

Smith, R. (1997), 'Self reflection and the self', in R. Porter (ed.), *Rewriting the Self: Histories from the Renaissance to the Present*. London: Routledge.

Speier, M. (1982), 'The everyday world of the child', in C. Jenks (ed.), *The Sociology of Childhood: Essential Readings*. London: Batsford Academic and Educational Limited.

Stainton Rogers, W. (2004), 'Promoting better childhoods: constructions of child concern', in M. J. Kehily (ed.), *An Introduction to Childhood Studies*. Maidenhead: Open University Press.

Sutherland, P. (1992), *Cognitive Development Today: Piaget and his Critics*. London: Paul Chapman Publishing Limited.

Taylor, C. (1989), *Sources of the Self: The Making of the Modern Identity*. Cambridge: Cambridge University Press.

Tomaselli, S. (1997), 'The death and rebirth of character in the eighteenth century', in R. Porter (ed.), *Rewriting the Self: Histories from the Renaissance to the Present*. London: Routledge.

Tucker, M. J. (1995), 'The child as beginning and end: 15th and 16th century English childhood', in L. deMause (ed.), *The History of Childhood*. Northvale, NJ: Jason Aronson Incorporated.

Tur, R. (1987), 'The "person" in law', in A. Peacocke and G. Gillett (eds), *Persons and Personality*. Oxford: Basil Blackwell Limited.

Turner, S. M. (1998), 'John Stuart Mill's children', in S. M. Turner and G. B. Matthews (eds), *The Philosopher's Child: Critical Perspectives in the Western Tradition*. Rochester, NY: University of Rochester Press.

Turner, S. M. and Matthews, G. B. (eds) (1998), *The Philosopher's Child: Critical Perspectives in the Western Tradition*. Rochester, NY: University of Rochester Press.

Verhellen, E. (2000), 'Children's rights and education', in A. Osler (ed.) (2000), *Citizenship and Democracy in Schools: Diversity, Identity, Equality*. Stoke-on-Trent: Trentham Books Limited.

Villa, D. (2001), *Socratic Citizenship*. Oxford: Princeton University Press.

Warnock, M. (1992), *The Uses of Philosophy*. Oxford: Blackwell Publishers.

Wiggins, D. (1976), 'Locke, Butler and the stream of consciousness', in A. O. Rorty (ed.), *The Identities of Persons*. Berkeley: University of California Press.

Wiggins, D. (1987), 'The person as object of science, as subject of experience, and as locus of value', in A. Peacocke and G. Gillett (eds), *Persons and Personality*. Oxford: Basil Blackwell Limited.

Williams, C. D. (1997), 'Another self in the case. Gender, marriage and the individual in Augustan literature', in R. Porter (ed.), *Rewriting the Self: Histories from the Renaissance to the Present*. London: Routledge.

Wilson, M. D. (ed.) (1969), *The Essential Descartes*. London: Penguin Books Limited.

Wintersberger, H. (1994), 'Costs and benefits – the economics of childhood', in J. Qvortrup, M. Bardy, G. Sgritta and H. Wintersberger (eds), *Childhood Matters: Social Theory, Practice and Politics*. Aldershot: Avebury.

Woodhead, M. (1997), 'Psychology and the cultural construction of children's needs', in A. James and A. Prout (eds), *Constructing and Reconstructing Childhood: Contemporary Issues in the Sociological Study of Childhood*. London: Falmer Press.

Wringe, C. A. (1981), *Children's Rights: A Philosophical Study*. London: Routledge & Kegan Paul Limited.

Zweig, A. (1998), 'Immanuel Kant's children', in S. M. Turner and G. B. Matthews (eds), *The Philosopher's Child: Critical Perspectives in the Western Tradition*. Rochester, NY: University of Rochester Press.

Index